J. V. & C. E. Spencer
123 Ennerdale Road
Newcastle upon Tyne
NE6 4DL
Tel. 0191 2620658

CW00450147

Hear Our Prayer

Raymond Chapman is Emeritus Professor of English in the University of London and a non-stipendiary priest in the Diocese of Southwark. He is Deputy Chairman of the Prayer Book Society and the author of many religious and literary titles, notably *Leading Intercessions* which has sold over 13, 000 copies.

Leading Intercessions

Widely praised and extensively used in churches that follow the three-year lectionary, *Leading Intercessions* is an invaluable worship resource which links the intercessions to the scripture readings of the day.

'Raymond Chapman's book . . . combines masterful use of language in succinct expression, a profound understanding of liturgical prayer within the context of Word and Sacrament and a depth of devotion that will encourage in the way of prayer all who use these prayers.'
Tufton Review

'beautifully written'
Church Times

'clear, dignified and appropriate for today. My deep hope is that people . . . will steal Raymond Chapman's words shamelessly.'
Andrew Burnham, *New Directions*

'sensitive and pastoral'
Church Observer

Hear Our Prayer

Gospel-based Intercessions for
Sundays, Holy Days
and Festivals – Years A, B and C

RAYMOND CHAPMAN

CANTERBURY
PRESS
Norwich

© Raymond Chapman 2003

First published 2003 by The Canterbury Press Norwich
(a publishing imprint of Hymns Ancient & Modern Limited,
a registered charity)
St Mary's Works, St Mary's Plain,
Norwich, Norfolk, NR3 3BH

www.scm-canterburypress.co.uk

British Library Cataloguing in Publication data

A catalogue record for this book is available from the British
Library

ISBN 1-85311-556-8

Typeset by Regent Typesetting, London
Printed and bound in Great Britain by
Biddles Ltd, *www.biddles.co.uk*

Contents

Introduction

The kind reception given to the previous volume *Leading Intercessions* has encouraged me to follow a similar pattern in this new collection of intercessory prayers. They are again designed for use with the Revised Common Lectionary.

These prayers are, however, composed on a different basis. Instead of finding a theme across all the readings for the day, I have drawn entirely on the Gospel passages. The accounts of the life and teaching of our Lord provide a pattern for all that we have in life and death. Whether we are concerned with worship, with global and local needs, with sickness and affliction or with the life to come, there is comfort and guidance in relating them to the written foundation record of our faith.

One of the strengths of the RCL is that a single Gospel is followed through each of the three years, with occasional readings from the Fourth Gospel. We become accustomed to the style and approach of each of the Evangelists, and this gives variety to the intercessions based on them. If only two of the other Sunday readings are used, and whichever Track is followed during Ordinary Time, the Gospel will always be read and will be the same in all churches. In the few instances where the Church of England has made different provision from the rest of the RCL, I have followed this reading, I hope without offence to the ecumenical intention of the whole book.

These prayers use images and phrases from the Gospel which will have been heard by the congregation a few minutes before the period of intercession. All present will be able to relate them to the petitions offered in prayer. It is the place in the Eucharist when the Ministry of the Word draws to its close before the

Offertory leads into the consecration of the gifts and the communion of the people. What has been proclaimed is brought into the life of the present and gathered towards the sacramental mystery.

If we base our intercessions on the Gospel, we are reminded of one of the most wonderful truths of the Christian faith. God knows our human condition and its needs not only through divine omniscience but by the direct experience of taking our nature in its sufferings and limitations. This is a deep mystery which makes us bold to relate our concerns closely to the life of Christ on earth.

The intercessions offered here are based on the Sunday readings for the Principal Service. Major Festivals like Christmas and Easter which have the same reading in each year are not repeated; otherwise there is something for every Sunday in each of the three years.

As well as the Sunday cycle, there are other days which are commonly observed during the year, and prayers are provided for these. There are also intercessions for special occasions, which can have wider application. For example, the order for a service with intention for the Guidance of the Holy Spirit would be appropriate for a Parochial Church Council or similar executive body, and prayers for the Sovereign could be used for any national celebration.

The structure of the intercessions

The fivefold division of subjects, which is widely used and has proved valuable in focussing attention, has been followed:

The Church As intercessions are usually offered within an act of public worship, and always on behalf of all Christians, we pray first for the Church as the

Body of Christ on earth and for Christ's people in their lives of service.

The world   This is the world which God created and Christ came to save. We pray for all human needs and that the lives of people and nations may fulfil the divine purpose. Our cares for the Church and for the world should never be formally separated, but we need to recognize the material preoccupations of secular society and to pray lovingly and without condescension.

The community   Next we move to the concerns that are most near to us: families, friends, neighbours, those with whom we work. Prayers for the wider world are often necessarily general, but here we can make our requests known more specifically. We pray too for all who live in the area that forms our local community, large or small. It is at this point that worshippers will also want to bring their personal lives before God and relate them to their social dimension.

The suffering   The compassion of God reaches out to all but is too often blocked by human sin and indifference. Those who suffer are particularly dear to him, and we offer our own sympathy and desire to help those, known or unknown to us, who are afflicted.

The communion of saints   Prayers for the dead have been part of Christian liturgy from the earliest years. Our remembrance of them draws us into the prayers of the whole Church, seen and unseen, in heaven and on earth. We recall our own mortality and affirm our faith in the resurrection to eternal life, and in the fellowship of all Christians, living and departed.

The intercessions can be offered in these sections, within a liturgical structure which invites congregational response, or as a continuous prayer. The breaks between sentences in each section give space for particular desires and concerns to be included, but the prayers can at any point be said without a break. The intercessor will usually wish to mention some specific needs. These are suggested words to help intercession and will often benefit from paraphrase or addition. For example, the word 'community' is often used in the third section and it may be more appropriate to say 'village', 'city', 'school' and so on.

For each occasion there is a brief invitation to prayer, based on the Gospel for the day, and a sentence to conclude the intercessions, gathering the petitions together and offering them through Jesus Christ whose words and deeds have just been recalled. These introductions and conclusions may suitably be said either by the celebrant or presiding minister or by the person leading the intercessions.

If the custom of the church is to use the second person singular *thou* form towards God, the words can readily be amended. Some care is needed in adapting the verbal forms to correspond. This is the preference of the author of this book, and indeed of many others, but both styles are now current.

Although the collection is envisaged largely for use in an act of public worship, it is hoped that it may be helpful also for smaller and more informal prayer groups. Further, it is suggested for individual use, to help intercession in personal prayers. Careful reading of the appointed Gospel passages may be followed by meditation and then intercession, not limited by what is here written but perhaps aided by it.

Intercessory prayer

Intercession at the Eucharist is a universal Christian tradition and has been observed since the earliest

liturgies. The Eucharist is principally a service of praise
and thanksgiving, culminating in the reception of the
sacramental elements of bread and wine. The liturgy
also includes instruction, penitence and intercession.
The prayers of intercession lead towards the supreme
moment of Christian worship and are united with the
very words of Christ at the Last Supper. They claim the
mercy of his Passion and atoning death and the power
of his Resurrection.

Intercession is only a part of prayer, but it is an
important one. The theology of intercessory prayer
may be complex, but the practice is an instinctive
response of faith and should be so addressed. Wherever
people are moved to pray, it is natural and right to ask
for blessing and strength in areas of concern. Christians
know that in such prayers we are not trying to change
the will of God for our own immediate benefit, or to
soften the heart of a remote and implacable tyrant.

It is enough to know that it is both our duty and our
privilege to bring the needs of individuals and communities before God in prayer. We have the command and
example of Christ, and the practice of the Church, to
assure us that this is a proper response of faith. It is one
of the many ways in which our natural desires are
accepted and sanctified. To lift people up in prayer is a
token both of our care for them and of our belief in the
love of God for all his creatures. In so doing, we are also
offering ourselves to be used in the furtherance of what
we ask. This is a vital element in intercession, whether
individual or on behalf of the whole congregation. As
we focus our concerns and make them articulate, we
come to realize how much they really mean to us. True
intercession is an offering of help as well as a plea for
help. It is a recognition that, although God needs
nothing from us, he graciously invites and accepts our
share in his loving purposes.

The author hopes and prays that this book may

indeed be useful to those who are charged with leading intercessions and also to those who wish to widen the intercessory element in their own prayers.

I am grateful for many appreciative responses to the previous book and for helpful suggestions. I particularly thank Christine Smith of the Canterbury Press for her foresight, advice and practical support.

Principal Service

Year A

FIRST SUNDAY OF ADVENT

Matthew 24:36–44

Let us pray, as we prepare for the coming of the Lord.

May the Church be faithful and vigilant, ever on guard against evil, and as a good servant ready for the Master's call . . . At this Advent time, grant to her ministers and all her people the grace to prepare in prayer and meditation for the coming Nativity.

Speak to a heedless world where many have ceased to learn from the past the signs of future danger . . . Be merciful to those who fail in the duty laid upon them for the guidance of others and open their eyes to follow the right path.

In all we do, in all our work, in our homes, in our times of quiet, let us so live that we are ready without fear for the call of God . . . Grant to those we love the grace of lives fitly offered.

Have mercy on those who have no future hope, those who value the passing moment beyond its worth, those who through pain and sorrow have ceased to care for what is to come . . . Give them the assurance that this present world is not the end.

We pray for those who have already been called to the future judgement and the future peace, for those who came with joyful expectation into the divine presence,

and for those who came bewildered and unprepared
. . . May the love of God enfold them all.

May our prayers be acceptable through Christ the Lord
who has come, is present here and will come again.

SECOND SUNDAY OF ADVENT

Matthew 3:1–12

Let us pray to God who receives all who come to him in
love and humility.

Renew the life of the Church, that her people shall hear
the call of the future and not rest in the comfort of the
past . . . May those whom the Lord has called be
confident in his mercy but not forgetful of his judgement.

Grant repentance to the nations of this world, for the
cleansing of what is false and evil, and the building of
what is true and good . . . Root out the complacency
that will not confess error and the indifference that
tolerates injustice.

Trusting in no achievements of our own, claiming no
privilege in the values of this world, may we and those
with whom we live and work, and all who share our
community, come to walk in the path of peace . . . Help
us to remember that we shall fulfil the will of God by
waiting upon his word.

Have mercy on all who think that their position sets
them above error and beyond judgement . . . Have
mercy also on those who are afraid to turn back to the
right way and are without hope.

May the departed find mercy at the heart of judgement

and be cleansed from all their sins so that they may stand perfect before the eternal majesty of God . . . Give us grace at this time to recollect that we too must die.

May Christ who knows the secrets of all hearts mercifully hear our prayers.

THIRD SUNDAY OF ADVENT

Matthew 3:1–12

Let us pray to God to open our lips to speak as messengers of his gospel.

May we who are the Church of Christ on earth hear his call to repentance . . . As we see the signs of his healing power, make us ready to receive him into our hearts at this time and to look for his coming in glory.

Come in mercy to the people who seek for help in the kingdoms of this world and do not look to the signs of the Kingdom of Heaven . . . Break through the doubt and uncertainty that cloud the vision, the false values that hide the truth, that all may know that salvation has come.

Make us faithful witnesses, to bring the knowledge of Christ into our homes, our work, our meeting with others . . . Guide all in this community so to seek that they may truly find.

Have mercy on the sick in body or mind, the disabled, the sorrowful. Lead them from the wilderness into the fertile land of your healing love, where they may be made whole.

Lord Christ who raised the dead, receive into your Kingdom the souls of the departed . . . As they saw the signs of your power in this world, may they enter into the fullness of your glory.

We offer our prayers through the one long expected who has come to be among us, Christ the Lord.

FOURTH SUNDAY OF ADVENT

Matthew 1:18–23

As we wait for the birth of the Lord, we pray for the Church and for the world he came to save.

Lord God, guide your Church into the way of truth and keep her free from false doctrine and all error . . . Give grace to her ministers, so that your purposes may be clearly known and faithfully proclaimed, to the glory of your name.

Come to the world where the truth is so often unknown and the message of hope not understood . . . Teach those who hold authority over others to govern without fear and suspicion and to seek the way of peace.

Bring into our homes the joy of those who trust in your love, and share that love with one another . . . Give light to families where love has turned to bitterness and jealousy. May the tender protection of Joseph and the gentleness of Mary be with them.

Have pity on all whose sleep is troubled, who lie awake in darkness or are tormented in their dreams . . . In the night hours, may the sick and those who watch with them know your calming presence and the assurance of your love.

Give rest to the departed and an awakening to heavenly joy . . . As you were with them in this life, so let them now be with you for ever, no longer afflicted by the doubts and fears that they once knew.

We offer our prayers in the name of Jesus our Emmanuel, God with us.

CHRISTMAS DAY

Luke 2:1–20 or John 1:1–14

Rejoicing in the precious gift of the Son, let us pray to the Lord.

Grant to the Church, illumined by the eternal light, the grace to shine as the servant of Incarnate God . . . May the simple faith of the shepherds, the adoration of the angels, and the love of the Holy Family be the ground of our worship and witness now and at all times.

Son of God, taking our human nature so that all broken humanity might be made new, look with mercy on a world which has not heeded the angelic message of peace . . . Bring to the nations knowledge of the love which has been from the beginning and which no sin can extinguish or folly destroy.

May the love that shone from the blessed manger bed be ours today . . . In every heart, every home, every place where some must work, may the grace and truth of God dwell with us and draw us into his holiness, and empower us to tell out the tidings of great joy.

Light of God, come into the darkness of pain and suffering . . . In the new day that has dawned, may the sick find healing, the sorrowful comfort, the despairing hope and the dying assurance . . . Bring the wanderers and the homeless to shelter . . . Shield the newly born and the mothers waiting for the time of birth.

Grant to the departed the peace that unites earth and heaven . . . The life that was in Christ, the life of all that was made, be theirs in the greater light of his eternal glory.

We offer our prayers through Christ, the Word made flesh for our salvation.

FIRST SUNDAY OF CHRISTMAS

Matthew 2:13–23

We pray to God who has shared the pain of the world.

May the Church, made an image of the glory of Christ, stand also as a witness to his suffering . . . Change our weakness into strength, our anxiety into trust that he who became helpless for love of us will be our present help and make us able to meet the needs of all who come.

In the world where many are driven from their homes as wanderers in strange lands, where tyrants rage and destroy the innocent, may God direct the ways of those who are lost in sorrow and fear . . . Come close to those who abuse their power, that they may learn to love, and turn from anger to compassion.

Give us grateful hearts for the security that we know, in our human lives and our assurance of the love of God . . . Grant to all in this community the mutual concern and sympathy which tell us that all grief is shared and is healed only by his presence.

We pray for those who have lost their homes and all who at the end of the day will have no place to rest . . . Bring them to a place of refuge, as Mary and Joseph were led to a home for their child . . . Comfort those who at this time are mourning for the death of children.

May those who died as little children find the fullness of life . . . May those who have died violently and unprepared find the peace that was denied them in their dying . . . May those who have killed come to repentance and pardon in their own deaths.

May our prayers be acceptable to the vulnerable Christ who is our Lord.

SECOND SUNDAY OF CHRISTMAS

John 1:1–18

Let us pray, trusting in God who receives all who come to him for grace.

As we have been granted the knowledge of God which comes only through the revelation of his Son, we pray that the Church may be a light to the world . . . Confident in truth and enabled by grace, may all her people tell with their lips and follow in their lives the new law of love. *L. IN YOUR M.*

Give to all people knowledge of the power of God who made the world and all that is in it . . . Grant humility to those who exercise human power, and give them right judgement in their decisions . . . Be merciful to those who do not know Christ or will not receive him, and let his light break through their darkness. *L. I Y M.*

Draw us closer to our families, our friends, our colleagues, with the love that has come into the world . . . Make us as those who are born again, not of human will but of God, the only source of life and the giver of grace. *L. Y M.*

Have mercy on all who are in error and guide them into the true light of Christ . . . Bring the fullness of life to those who have made their lives narrow by rejecting love . . . Comfort and heal the sick and all who suffer, and strengthen with grace those who care for them.

Hold in eternal life the faithful departed who have witnessed to the truth of Christ in this world . May the light which led them on their way shine on them as perpetual light and make them perfect by his grace.

We pray in the name of Christ in whom we have received grace upon grace.

THE EPIPHANY

Matthew 2:1–12

Let us kneel in homage as we pray to God, the King of Kings.

We offer our richest gifts of prayer and praise, knowing them imperfect but trusting in the holiness of Christ to make them holy . . . As the Wise Men were led by a star to Bethlehem, so guide your pilgrim Church to worship in holiness and bow down in adoration until the time when your purpose is accomplished.

Give wisdom to the rulers of this world, that they may see the light of truth and follow the way of peace . . . Let them not be moved by fear or envy; make them ready to see you in what seems small and unimportant, so that their power is used not in pride but in service.

As we have known the joy of Christmas and rejoiced in the gift of the Holy Child, may we now bring to him our gifts of love and reverence . . . Make our lives, in our families and in all our meeting with others, tokens of the treasures that in our hearts we offer to the Lord.

Look with mercy on those whose journeys through the
world are long and who can see no guiding star . . .
Bring them through the hard places of sickness and
sorrow until they may set down their burdens and rest
. . . Give grace to those who are seeking truth and
cannot find their way: lead them to the feet of Christ.

Receive the souls of the departed into the Kingdom
where all journeys end and all worship is fulfilled in
glory . . . As little Bethlehem was made great by the
divine birth, so may those who were humble and
unregarded in this world be numbered with the saints
in heaven.

We make our offering of prayer to Christ, King, Priest
and atoning Sacrifice.

THE BAPTISM OF CHRIST (FIRST SUNDAY OF EPIPHANY)

Matthew 3:1–17

Let us pray to God who in baptism has called us to be
his body on earth.

Send the Holy Spirit upon the Church, that the glory of
the Son may be known and proclaimed . . . Bless all who
come for baptism, fill them with grace to walk in the
way of Christ whose example they have followed. Bless
those who are leading people to know the Lord.

Cleanse with the water of holiness all that is corrupt in
the world today. Speak with the voice from heaven to
those in authority and lead them into the right way . . .
Teach them that all their power comes from one who is
greater than they, the source of all power.

Bless all those who at this time are preparing for baptism, for themselves or for their children . . . Give them the light of the Holy Spirit, to lead them to new life in Christ . . . May all that we do in our daily lives be pleasing in the sight of God.

Be with those for whom the glory is veiled by suffering and let the light of heaven shine upon them again . . . As Christ followed the way of human obedience, so may he bring healing to the sick and comfort to the sorrowful.

Let the heavens be opened to those who have passed from this world . . . Cleansed by baptism and kept faithful by the Holy Spirit, may they find all joy and peace in the glory of the Father.

We pray in the name of Christ, the Son, the Beloved.

SECOND SUNDAY OF EPIPHANY

John 1:29–42

Let us pray to God, who guides all who seek him in faith.

As you have called your chosen ones to be your witnesses, give power to the Church to witness faithfully . . . Since by grace we have known the true Messiah, may we make him known to others . . . As the first disciples followed Christ to his dwelling, so may his servants at this time come to him and rest with him.

Bless the people of this world with wisdom to know the Lord and the will to follow him . . . Holy Spirit, descending on him and abiding in him, enter into the dark places of the world, to banish ignorance and reveal the Saviour who has come.

As Andrew brought his brother to Christ, so may we bring to him those who are close to us but do not yet know the fullness of his love . . . May he come into our homes and make them his own . . . May he, the great Teacher, give light to all who teach and all who learn in this community.

Have mercy on those who seek rest and cannot find it; give them hope in Christ who calls the seekers to find their peace in him . . . Come to the lonely ones who have no one to walk with them and show them the way . . . May they find human friendship, and divine love.

Grant eternal rest to those who have come at last to where Christ dwells in glory . . . As they have sought him and tried to serve him in this world, may they see him with full vision and abide in him for ever.

We pray in the name of Christ, the Lamb of God who takes away the sin of the world.

THIRD SUNDAY OF EPIPHANY

Matthew 4:12–20

Let us pray to God who has called us to his service.

Give to the Church a burning zeal to win souls for Christ . . . Empower the shared ministry of all believers, so that human love may serve the love of God and make it known . . . Let your people never be deaf when you call them to your work, whether it is great or little.

May the people who sit in darkness see the great light of God and know his presence among them . . . Bless all our work in this world, but help us to know that it is not the whole of life . . . Enrich the skills and talents of daily labour, opening them to new service for the Kingdom.

Be present with our families and all the families of this community . . . Increase our love for one another but save us from the clinging selfishness that will not share our security with those who have none . . . When we are called to be apart from one another, keep us confident that we are not separated from your protecting love.

Come close to those who have had to leave their homes and loved ones . . . Comfort parents who are lonely when children have gone away . . . As the disciples were given the power of healing, bless all those who care for the sick in mind or body.

Receive into the heavenly light those who have passed through the shadow of death . . . Healed of all their infirmity, may they rejoice with those who first heard the call of Jesus and walked with him in Galilee.

We pray in the name of Christ, the source of all strength to those who hear his call.

FOURTH SUNDAY OF EPIPHANY

John 2:1–11

Let us pray to God who gives freely and beyond measure.

May God who knows the secrets of all hearts and who hears the prayers of all who turn to him in their need, give strength to his Church . . . We pray that from the weakness of our mortal nature we may draw out the good wine of the gospel, that we may drink of it and bring new life to others.

Come with mercy to the world where so many are anxious about the needs of every day . . . Give assurance to those who are in doubt, that they may trust in your will to provide, and may offer their resources to the aid of those in need.

We pray for those recently married or preparing for their weddings . . . Give them joy in each other, faithfulness in their lives together and the support of their families and friends . . . May Christ bless all families with his presence.

Bless those who have too little for their needs and fear for what is to come . . . Teach them to ask with faith and to follow where they are led, that they may find the good gifts that are in God's love.

We pray for those whose hour has come, who have passed from the anxieties and pleasures of this world . . . May they receive the good wine that is kept to the last, in the heavenly feast where Christ the gracious guest is the host of all who have put their trust in him.

May Christ whose glory has been revealed that we may believe, accept our prayers.

THE PRESENTATION OF CHRIST

Luke 2:22–40

Let us pray, as we are commanded by the Law of God.

Give to the Church the spirit of prophecy, to proclaim the light that has come to lighten all nations . . . As Mary and Joseph made their offering according to the Law, so may all Christian people offer their prayer and praise for the gift of the Son according to his new law of love.

Let all people know that the day of salvation has come and the love of God reaches out to the ends of the earth

. . . May those who administer justice understand that all law and power come from God, to be offered back to him with humility . . . Give grace to all who teach, that they may be guided in wisdom and insight.

As Jesus found the shelter of an earthly home in Nazareth, may his presence bless our homes and all the families in our community . . . Bless those who rejoice in a new birth . . . Be with our older people and grant them still the bright vision of divine love.

Have mercy on parents whose hearts are pierced by the loss or suffering of their children . . . May the light that was brought by the Son of God be their light in the time of darkness . . . Bless those who are near to death, that they may be sustained by the sight of salvation.

We pray for those who have departed in peace from this world and entered into the greater life . . . May the light of heaven shine perpetually upon them, in the realm where the secrets of all hearts are revealed.

We pray in the name of Christ, our light and our salvation.

EPIPHANY 5 (PROPER 1)

Matthew 5:13–20

Let us pray to the Lord who has called us to be faithful in his service.

Give to the Church power to proclaim your great works and to shine as a light that will draw all people to love and honour your name . . . May your people never lose by sin or negligence the holiness which is given to all who trust in you and seek to do your work.

As people seek their own ways and turn away from

obedience, bring them to know that the Law of God is strong and does not change as human fashions change . . . Give courage to any who have gifts which they do not know, or which they have failed to use, and lead them into the light of the divine purpose fulfilled.

Bless those who do the work of God in our community, who tend the sick in mind or body and bring aid to the infirm . . . May they have strength to continue, and may they be an example, that others shall follow in the paths of mercy.

Look with compassion on all who have lost the assurance of faith and purpose in life which they once had . . . May they know that they are not cast out from your love but may be won back to the way that cannot be found by human will alone . . . Bless those who in sickness and distress still shine brightly in their patient trust.

Receive into glory the souls of those whose light shone as a witness in the world, and have mercy on those whose light was darkened by sin or suffering . . . May they too shine with the light that cannot be extinguished, and find the peace that they did not find here.

We pray in the name of Christ, in whom all the commandments are fulfilled.

EPIPHANY 6 (PROPER 2)

Matthew 5:21–37

Let us pray to the Lord who has given us a new and greater Law.

Give grace to the Church to follow the commands of the gospel, and to teach them so that all may serve in faith and obedience . . . Cleanse us from anger, strife and impurity, and empower us to fulfil the example of Christ, in firm resolve and gentle compassion.

Guide into peace a world where there is so much hatred and bitterness, where the power of law is used for revenge and gain, where hurtful words are spoken in scorn . . . Forgive the breaches of trust, the false promises, the anger which breeds its own destruction . . . Open the way of reconciliation to the minds that are closed against it.

Wherever disputes threaten the harmony of our homes, where there is hostility towards neighbours, where tension is growing in places of work, teach us to forgive and to acknowledge our own mistakes . . . Shield us from careless speaking in moments of stress.

Have mercy on all whose lives have been broken by quarrels with those they have loved . . . Bring healing to the marriages that are falling apart, and comfort where relationships have failed . . . Grant that those who are in legal difficulties may be relieved and find mercy in the course of justice.

May the departed find rest in the new life where all anger is ended, all injuries forgiven, all damaged hearts made whole . . . As we remember that promise of glory, let its light shine on our lives in this world and be our guide.

May our prayers be accepted in the name of Christ, in whom alone we may be reconciled.

EPIPHANY 7 (PROPER 3)

Matthew 5:38–48

Let us pray as the children of one heavenly Father.

Fill the Church with the love that does not come from agreement and fellowship alone but reaches out to embrace those who are hostile and scornful . . . Let no task seem too heavy, no forgiving gesture too costly, because all is done in the strength of God who pardons and saves to the uttermost and has made us his messengers here on earth.

Correct in mercy the errors which divide people into friends and enemies . . . Heal all divisions which set nations, races, religions in opposition to one another . . . Cleanse the world of all the darkness which seeks revenge and claims that it is justice.

May the love that is in our homes never become narrow and excluding, but let it reach out to all who can be drawn into our care . . . Make the life of this community a token that we are all children of one Father, and bless its members who patiently serve those who are in need.

Have mercy on those who suffer because of faults that have not been forgiven, and those who do not know how to forgive but are caught up in a cycle of retaliation . . . Give peace and a fresh start to those who are weighed down by guilt, because they have failed in love and generosity and do not know how to make amends.

Pardon in their last hour those who die unreconciled and still bearing a load of anger . . . May they too be numbered with your children whose deaths were peaceful and all be blessed together in everlasting life.

Christ give us grace to offer our prayers in love for all people.

SECOND SUNDAY BEFORE LENT

Matthew 6:25–34

Let us pray to God, the giver of all beauty in heaven and earth.

Inspire your Church with zeal to seek the Kingdom, setting aside all worldly concerns that may lead away from the goal . . . Let your people live each day as if it were the first and the last of your purpose for us, to make known the righteousness which is not our own but the fruit of your bounty.

As we give thanks for beauty of the natural world, we pray that it may not be lost through human greed and folly . . . May those who have control of change act responsibly, as knowing that they are stewards of a treasure not of their making, a glory beyond the riches of the kings and rulers of the earth.

When troubles come in our lives and we are concerned for ourselves or those near to us, make us free from the anxiety that destroys hope and show us the way that is opening before us . . . Confident in the love that sustains what love had created, let us seek to do your will in all things.

Comfort those who are weighed down by worry about food and clothing and other bodily needs . . . Help the individuals and the agencies working for the relief of poverty and give generous compassion to all who have enough to spare for others.

Bless in your nearer presence those who have ended

their span of life and entered into beauty beyond anything they knew upon earth . . . May they find peace in
the Kingdom where anxiety has gone and there is no
more fear, because God's righteousness is all in all.

We pray through Christ who has taught us to trust and
not to be afraid.

SUNDAY NEXT BEFORE LENT

Matthew 27:1–9

Let us pray to God who leads us to see his glory and
hear his voice.

As the Church has been called to be the servant of your
glory, may she be worthy to be your dwelling on earth
. . . It is good for us to be here, and we pray that we may
be filled with the wisdom of the Law, the vision of the
Prophets and the grace of Jesus Christ now and in all
time to come.

Bless the people of the world with the light that leads
them to the heights where they may see your glory, and
the strength to return to the plain where the work of life
must go on . . . Guide those in authority to hear the
wisdom of the past and to see with clear vision where
their present duty lies.

As we go about our daily lives, grant us the times of
peace when we may be aware of the glory that is all
around us . . . Through our prayers and meditations
bring us closer to the Saviour, to follow him as the first
disciples followed, and to know his fullness as they
knew it.

Have mercy on those whose suffering lets them see
only the darkness of the cloud and keeps them from

hearing the voice of divine assurance . . . Dispel the fear that holds many back from knowing that God is love and calls us to draw near and adore him.

May those who have died in the faith of Christ, and in this world received a partial vision of his glory, now enter into the fullness of his presence . . . May they dwell for ever in the holy place from which the blessed ones are never turned away.

May our prayers be accepted through Christ, the Son revealed in glory.

ASH WEDNESDAY

John 8:1–11

In penitence and faith, let us pray to the Lord.

As we begin this season of Lent, may our offering of prayer and abstinence be secret, and our love and compassion in the name of Christ be manifest . . . Grant to the Church the spirit of true repentance and the joy that breaks through sorrow when sins repented become sins forgiven.

Bring to a world where many trust in material things and seek their goal in greater wealth the knowledge of where the true treasure is to be found . . . Enlighten those whose confidence is in themselves, to know that even if their works are good they are rich only in offering them to God.

Help us now to consider our relationships with others, to see where we can put right the faults we have committed and to heal trust that has been broken . . . Open our hearts to receive the treasure of God which comes to us through the treasure of human love.

Have mercy on the poor who have no riches to give, no luxury to set aside . . . May this Lent be a time of greater understanding and care towards those in need . . . Bring relief to the hungry whose fasting is not chosen but forced upon them.

Grant that the faithful departed may find the heavenly treasure that they sought during their lives on earth . . . We rejoice with them that their years of obedience and devotion have come to their end in the eternal worship of God.

We pray in the name of Christ, our example and our strength in all our Lenten offerings.

FIRST SUNDAY OF LENT

Matthew 4:1–11

Let us pray for God's protection of the Church and of the world.

Guard the Church against the assaults of evil . . . Be close to us when we are tempted to abuse the gifts we have received, to make a show of strength or to use influence from false motives . . . May we never use means we know to be wrong, with the excuse that the end will be good.

Look with mercy on a world where there are many temptations: where some think only of their own bodily comfort, some desire to show their power by foolish acts, some seek greater power and embrace evil to attain it . . . Come with your saving love and bring life to the desert places of all hearts.

Grant that what we offer in this Lent may not become a temptation to pride . . . May our homes be made more joyful and our work more dedicated as we seek to bring our lives closer to the life of our Saviour.

Have mercy on those who in the wilderness of the world find no relief . . . Hungry, fearful, lonely, many are falling into despair or following ways that lead to deeper distress . . . May God and his angels bring them relief.

We pray for those who have passed from this world and are free from all temptation . . . We give thanks that they are delivered from evil, and pray that we in our time may be brought to worship with them and with the host of angels.

May our prayers be accepted in the name of Christ, tempted like us but without sin.

SECOND SUNDAY OF LENT

John 3:1–17

In the power of the Spirit, let us pray to God.

Renew your Church by the working of the Holy Spirit . . . In quiet and humble rebirth may your people find new strength as your body in the world and show the way of salvation to all who seek.

 God who loved the world even to sending the Son to be its Saviour, come among us for the healing of conflict between nations and races . . . Draw those who hold power and influence into the presence of Christ, to know his love and to make it their own in all their dealings.

Lift up our eyes to see the grace of God in all around us . . . Lift up our hearts to be his messengers to our

families and friends and in our community . . . Help us
to find in what is familiar the new birth of his love.

Have mercy on those who have lost their way and no
longer seek to know God and to do his will . . . May the
life-governing Spirit bring healing to the sick, and
strength to those who minister to them.

May the souls of those who have died be gloriously
born again to the eternal life where love is complete
and the night of seeking turns to the perfect day . . . May
we too in our time be born again in glory.

We pray in the name of Christ, lifted up in pain and in
triumph for our sake.

THIRD SUNDAY OF LENT

John 4:5–42

Let us pray to God who knows the secrets of all hearts.

May the Lord who gives the living water to all who
come to him in faith, give grace to the Church, so to
drink of that water that she may bring life to many . . .
May he lift our eyes to see where the time is ripe for
harvest and seek to be worthy labourers for the coming
of the Kingdom.

Give the word of truth to the world, where there is
strife between nations and races, where faiths can be
hostile and gender divisive . . . May honesty overcome
all shame and deceit, so that wrongs that have been
hidden may be brought to light and healed.

May our Lord be with us in our homes and in all the
homes of this community, to teach us by his word, to
sustain us with the food of loving obedience and lead

us to worship in spirit and in truth . . . Make us honest
in our dealings with one another and repentant for our
sins.

Have mercy on all whose lives are distressed by broken
relationships, by misunderstandings that have turned
to bitterness, by the suppressed anxiety that eats away
the heart . . . May those who have found only partial
truth be led into the right way, to know and to perform
the will of God.

May those who have passed from this world, and now
drink of the living water that flows from the throne of
God, rejoice in the eternal worship which is beyond all
place and time . . . May we by grace come to the same
rejoicing.

We pray in the name of Christ, the Messiah of all who
worship in spirit and truth.

FOURTH SUNDAY OF LENT

John 9:1–41

Let us pray to God for light and healing in the Church
and in the world.

Give to the Church the perfect vision of truth and the
will to serve it . . . Open the eyes of the faithful to the
faults that hinder their ministry, so that the light may
shine through them to the glory of God.

Lighten the darkness of the world where so many
stumble and fall in the blindness of pride, of false trust,
of power misused . . . When people doubt the divine
love and meet with suspicion the signs of its working,
let the words of those who have known it be heard
above the voices of mistrust.

Give to our families and to all the homes of this community the love that remains faithful in adversity and does not fear when hostility comes from outside . . . In all our meeting with others, may we speak the truth with boldness and witness to the blessings that we have received.

Have mercy on all who are blind or whose sight is failing . . . Empower and guide those who work to treat afflictions of the eyes, and bless their skill . . . Give courage to parents whose children have sight problems, and bless their acts of care and love.

We pray for the departed whose sins have been washed away and who live now in the light of heaven that will never fade . . . Grant that we may come to share with them the perfect vision of God.

May our prayers be accepted in the name of Christ, the light of the world.

or MOTHERING SUNDAY

Luke 2:33–35

Let us pray for the Church and the world, cherished in the tender love of God.

As our Lord grew to manhood under a mother's care, may his Church be as a mother to her children . . . Bless her ministers with the gift of compassion, to offer themselves in service to all who come to seek their help.

We pray for the world, that all its people may be as one family in harmony and peace . . . Let motherly love be the desire and the ideal of all the human race . . . Bless those in positions of power, that they may seek to serve and protect those under their authority.

Bless our homes with care and concern for one another
. . . May our families be as the Holy Family in shared
love and worship . . . Be ever close with the gift of
your unfailing love to the mothers and children in our
community.

Have mercy on the mothers who are in distress, those
who have lost children through death or estrangement,
those whose children are sick in body or mind . . . Grant
them strength in their affliction and healing for those
they love.

We pray for the departed who have known human love
on earth and have passed into the divine love of heaven
. . . May they be in peace and joy with blessed Mary and
all the saints.

We pray in the name of Christ, who loves us as a
mother loves her children.

FIFTH SUNDAY OF LENT

John 11:1–45

Let us pray to God whose word is the word of life.

As Thomas and the other disciples followed their Lord
in faith, give to your people the trust in him that takes
away all fear . . . As Mary and Martha saw with their
human eyes his power of resurrection, let your Church
witness to his risen presence among us.

Have mercy on a world where many do not follow the
way of life but choose the dark way that leads to the
death of hope . . . May those in high places know that
their power is limited and that all authority comes only
from the Lord of life, the conqueror of death.

Bless our families, friends and neighbours when they

*SEP BY DISTANCE, work
sick*

are in distress and doubt . . . Keep us faithful to one
another and to our Lord . . . Help us to trust in his word
and to obey his commands even when the way forward
is not clear to us.

Look with pity on those who mourn, especially those
who feel no hope of resurrection . . . Strengthen all   *Yes
who walk in fear but are loyal to their calling . . . Deal   mind.*
tenderly with those who are at the point of death, and
ease their passing.

God, in whom the dead are alive and shall never die
again, receive the souls of the faithful departed . . . As
their bodies lie in the grave, grant them eternal life in
Christ, whose word they trusted in their time on earth.

We pray in the name of Christ, the Resurrection and the
Life.

MERCIFUL FATHER

PALM SUNDAY

Matthew 21:1–11

Let us pray for the Church and for the world, to the
Lord, the King of Glory.

As the Church rejoices in the triumphal entry of our
Lord, grant to us also the spirit of repentance, and
sorrow for his suffering . . . May we at this holy time set
forward the message of his salvation and lay our minds
and wills before him as an offering of faith.

Bring to a world that judges by outward signs of power
the wisdom to discern where true power lies in humility and love . . . Open the eyes of the rulers of the
nations to see the one true King and be ready to serve at
his command.

Give to us and to all those around us the vision of

holiness in the daily scene of work and play . . . Help us
to find in those we too easily take for granted the image
of Christ the Lord, and to honour one another as those
who seek to follow in his way.

Have mercy on the sick and suffering for whom the
shadow of the Cross is plainer at this time than the
glory of the day and who call out not in triumph but in
anguish . . . Give them relief in their affliction and the
hope of new life.

May the voices of those who bore witness to God in this
world now be blended with the eternal praise of the
angels in heaven . . . May theirs be the song of triumph
over sin and death.

We offer our prayers in the name of Christ who has
come to save his people.

MAUNDY THURSDAY

John 13:1–17, 31b–35

In love and humility, let us pray to God for the Church
and for the world.

Cleanse the Church from all impurity that would harm
her witness . . . Give to all her members the spirit of
mutual love that reaches out to the whole world . . .
Make us ever faithful in celebrating and receiving the
holy sacrament of the Lord's Supper.

Give grace to all who hold authority, to become as
those who serve and to care more for the needs of those
they rule than for their own status and power . . . Let all
live together in peace, free from deceit and betrayal,
keeping one holy fellowship.

Sanctify our meals together, that they may follow the

pattern of Christ and his disciples who sat together on the night before he suffered . . . Help us to draw more of our acquaintance to share in the communion of believers.

Come with healing to those whose feet are stained and weary with the sins and sorrows of life . . . Make them clean, bring them peace, feed them with the love of Christ so that they may again find love in their own hearts.

We join our worship with those who were strengthened by the sacrament on earth and have taken their place at the heavenly banquet . . . Grant to us so to walk in love that we may come as those cleansed from all impurity to the throne of grace.

We make our prayers in the name of Christ who makes his people clean.

GOOD FRIDAY

John 18:1—19:42

In the sorrow and the glory of the Passion, let us pray to the Lord.

At the foot of the Cross we offer the prayers of the Church . . . May his people proclaim the death of Jesus Christ through word and sacrament, through teaching and example . . . May we be worthy to stand with Mary his Mother and the Beloved Disciple and know the price of our salvation.

We pray for the world that Christ died to save . . . As he was crucified outside the city, may his healing power enter the places where there is ignorance and indifference this day . . . May our fallen humanity be cleansed and renewed by the blood and water of his last hour.

In our homes and in our work, draw us closer together and teach us how to bear each other's burdens . . . Be with all in this community who this day must work or who seek only their own pleasure, and bring them to understand the pain that was borne for them.

Comfort and heal those who stand in the shadow of death, the mothers who have seen their children die, the friends who have been separated by death, all who are dying at this time . . . Grant that those whose crosses are heavy may find new hope in the Cross of Christ.

We remember those who have died with Christ and have passed with him from darkness to light . . . Keep us mindful of our own mortality, that in our last hour we may find peace and assurance in the Cross.

Christ died for us: we trust in him alone, and pray in his name.

EASTER EVE

Matthew 27:57–66

As the memory of the Passion draws towards the joy of the Resurrection, let us pray in quiet confidence.

Now let the Church, born from sorrow and despair to a glorious hope, rest with Christ in the tomb and prepare for the day of Resurrection . . . As his violated body was received with loving care, so may the body of his faithful now on earth honour him with humility and reverence in their worship.

Bring to the world, so torn with violence and destruction, an ending of strife, and grant the peace that can heal its wounds . . . Give to the rich and powerful the spirit of compassion; bring relief to those who have nothing.

Grant to us and our families a time to pause and prepare for the celebration of our risen Lord . . . To all in this community, as they take their time of recreation, bring the true meaning of the day, to share the love that Jesus received from his friends in death.

Give grace to those who tend the sick and the injured, who care for the damaged minds and the broken bodies . . . Have mercy on all who need their help, and on those who are now dying, that the bed of death may be a bed of hope and peace.

Have mercy on those who have left their earthly bodies and come in spirit to the Kingdom that will not pass away . . . May Christ, who has gone before through the shadow of death, raise them up into light and life eternal.

We pray in the name of Jesus Christ who in love for us entered the darkness of the tomb.

EASTER DAY

Matthew 28:1–10

As disciples who know that Christ is risen, let us pray for the Church and for the world.

As your Church rejoices this day in the Resurrection of her Lord and Saviour, may her worship be reverent and her proclamation faithful . . . May every Christian soul respond in faith to the call of the Master and make haste to tell the good news.

Let the Easter hope be known in all the world . . . Give light to those who seek, assurance to those who doubt, and peace to all . . . May Christ be known as the only Lord, the only hope of the nations.

Be with our families and friends and all who share with us the wonderful day of Resurrection . . . May the presence of Christ bring us close to those who are separated from us, in the knowledge that no distance can part us from his love.

Have mercy on those who stand at the open door of faith but are held back by doubt or fear of their unworthiness . . . Draw them in, that they may begin the new life that Christ has brought . . . Help and comfort those for whom suffering and sorrow mar the happiness of this day.

We pray for those who, having shared with Christ the death of the body, now share with him the eternal life of his Resurrection . . . May the promise that has been fulfilled in them be our hope in this world and our place in the world to come.

We pray in the name of Christ who conquered death that we might live for ever.

SECOND SUNDAY OF EASTER

John 20:19–31

In the power of the Spirit, let us pray for grace to do the works of faith.

Grant to the Church, the gathered people of the gospel, wisdom to know and power to proclaim the good news of the Resurrection . . . Make her ministers strong in the Holy Spirit to bring pardon and healing in the name of Christ.

We pray for a world where many wish to believe but are held back by doubt . . . Open the way to the freedom that is in Christ, that his peace may prevail among the nations and in the hearts of all people.

Grant to us, our families, friends and neighbours, the grace of the Resurrection . . . Break through the closed doors of our fear and doubt and give us the faith that needs no sign but the knowledge of divine love present among us.

Have mercy on all who suffer persecution for their faith, who must meet in secret and cannot worship openly . . . Give them strength in their need, give light to those who oppress them, so that all who trust in the Resurrection may be free to share their joy.

We pray for the departed who trusted their Lord in this world and now see him in the fullness of his glory . . . May their sins be forgiven and may we who now follow in faith share with them the promised blessing.

We pray in the name of Christ, by whose wounds we are healed.

THIRD SUNDAY OF EASTER

Luke 24:13–35

Let us pray to the Lord revealed to us in word and sacrament.

Help your people to search the Scriptures to bring us nearer to our Lord . . . May the hearts of Christians burn with faith as they feel his presence . . . Help us to know and to make him known in the breaking of bread.

Guide the feet that walk in doubt and uncertainty and have lost their way on the long roads of the world . . . Dispel the anxieties and the false reports that keep people apart: set them free with the good news of salvation.

May Christ be the guest at every table . . . May we see him in the stranger as well as in those close to us and make the weary and hungry welcome for his sake.

We pray for the homeless and for those who wander without a destination . . . Grant shelter to the unprotected, bread to the hungry and rest to the weary . . . Bless those who do the work of relief at home and abroad.

Be with those whose day is far spent and who are near to death . . . We pray for those who are with Christ in the eternal feast of his love and see him with the eyes of perfect sight.

We pray in the name of Christ, our companion through every day.

FOURTH SUNDAY OF EASTER

John 10:1–10

Let us pray for faithful following of the will of God.

Guard the Church from false teaching and from all error . . . Lead your pilgrim people in the right way to follow their Lord through the gate that leads to abundant life, and in turn to lead others to find the way.

Shield the peoples of this world against those that would destroy the innocent and lead astray the ignorant . . . Grant wisdom to discern and follow the true way, to find the fullness of living which is God's will for all his creation.

Make us good shepherds in places where we may have influence, helping our families, friends and neighbours and those with whom we work . . . Bless all who are leaders in our community and grant them grace to work for the common good.

Have mercy on those who have lost their way through bad advice and false teaching . . . Restore to them the abundant life that is in Christ, and may his voice bring peace and healing to their wounded souls.

We pray for those who have passed through the gate of death and entered into eternal life . . . We rejoice with them in the promise of life more abundant than this world can give, where Christ calls his flock to be with him in glory.

May our prayers be accepted in the name of Christ, the Good Shepherd of his sheep.

FIFTH SUNDAY OF EASTER

John 14:1–14

Let us pray in faith to God for the Church and for the world.

Grant that the Church may always follow in the way of Christ, proclaim his truth and live his risen life . . . Keep Christian people in knowledge and service of the Father, that his will may be done on earth as it is in heaven.

As the disciples were led to understand and taught to seek God in prayer, so may those who are counted wise in the world learn where true wisdom is to be found . . . Teach those in positions of authority to know that all earthly power is given from above.

When our hearts are troubled, bless us with faith to offer strength and assurance in our homes and in our work . . . Bless those in this community who help by teaching or example to bring people to know God and to walk in his ways.

Hear the prayers of those who cry out for relief in their afflictions, in sickness, poverty, loneliness, uncertainty . . . Grant them the assurance that Christ, who has gone before them through suffering to glory, is near to them and will bring them home.

We pray for the departed who have come to the place which Christ has prepared for them, where they shall be with him for ever . . . We pray that we may so follow him in this world that we too shall be gathered into the Father's house.

We pray in the name of Christ the Way, the Truth and the Life.

SIXTH SUNDAY OF EASTER

John 14:15–21

Let us pray in confidence to the Father who has sent us the Spirit to be our Advocate.

Grant that the Church, guided by the Spirit of Truth, may keep and declare the commandments of God . . . May we so live in the divine love that the Spirit will live in us and be our guide.

Lord of the world, where by many Christ is not seen and the Spirit is not known, do not leave your children as orphans without hope . . . Bless those who have rule over others, and lead them into the way of truth, that the nations may be healed and your praise declared to the ends of the earth.

With the eyes of faith, may we see Christ in our families, our friends and neighbours and all we meet . . . Help us to live as he has commanded, to know his love, and to be the channels of the Spirit in our community.

We pray for those who have no comfort, for the lonely and all who feel themselves to be without a guide . . . Have pity on children who are orphans, all who are neglected and abused, and give them the protecting love that will bring them new lives.

We pray for those who have sought to live by the truth in this world and now are brought to truth in its fullness . . . We rejoice with them that they abide for ever with God, to be his children in the light of heaven.

We pray in the name of Christ who reveals himself to those who love him.

ASCENSION DAY

Luke 22:44–53

Rejoicing in the glorious Ascension, let us pray to the Lord.

Make your Church a messenger of the gospel that has been revealed, and a witness to all nations of Christ, the highly exalted . Keep all Christian people open to receive the power of the Holy Spirit, the giver of life.

Now let all nations know that Christ is ascended in glory . Bless the missionaries and teachers who work to make him known . . . As his humanity is taken up into heaven, may the perfect image of God be restored to all humankind.

As we look up to heaven in adoration, let us turn our eyes also towards the needs that lie around us . . . Make us bearers of your word to those who share our lives, witnesses to our community of the divine glory.

Have mercy on those who cannot see beyond the clouds of sorrow and pain that cover them, and those whose vision is darkened by guilt without relief . Grant them the knowledge of Christ who has borne our suffering and made atonement for sin, to fill them with his light.

We pray for the departed who have followed where Christ has led and been lifted up to be with him in heaven. We pray that he will receive us to himself when he shall come again.

May our prayers be accepted through Christ, risen, ascended, glorified.

SEVENTH SUNDAY OF EASTER

John 17:1–11

Let us pray to God, Lord of the Church and of the world.

We pray for the people of your Church, those you have called to hear and believe your word . . . Draw them together in unity, inspired by the mutual love of the Father and the Son to be as one in faith and hope and love.

For all the people of the world that Christ came to save, those who acknowledge his power and those who do not know him, we ask that his glory may shine upon them and make them his own . . . As he has authority over all, may those who exercise power learn the way of his justice and his mercy.

Protect those whom you have given us in love to be our families and friends . . . Guide them with the grace promised to all who are your own, and help us to spread by word and example the knowledge of your glory.

Come tenderly to those who having heard and sought to follow have fallen away and lost the vision that once they knew . . . Bring them back to the way that leads to eternal life . . . Have mercy on the sick, grant them healing and renewal of life.

We remember those who in this world began their eternal life through faith and have entered into its fullness . . . As they are now in your presence, so may we grow in grace towards that vision of glory.

We pray in the name of Christ, glorified before all worlds.

PENTECOST

John 20:19–23

In the power of the Spirit, let us pray to the Lord.

Guide the Church, blessed with the gift of the Holy Spirit, to preach the gospel to all nations . . . Give to your people words of power, words of comfort, words of life . . . Bless your ministers and all who preach the way of salvation.

God who has spoken to the world, to be heard and praised in many tongues, speak now to a world troubled by divisions and failures to understand . . . Break down the barriers that hold people apart, so that your wonderful works shall be known.

May we be granted a share in the gifts of the Spirit bestowed on the Apostles, to guide us in sharing the good news with our families and neighbours and all whose lives touch our own . . . Inspire us with the breath of life and the fire of love.

Have mercy on all whose lives are so limited by poverty, suffering or ignorance that they do not know the fullness of life that is your will for them . . . May the Holy Spirit come to them, to be their Comforter and lead them into light.

We pray for those whose lives were led by the Spirit of God and who now rejoice where human tongues have ceased, to praise him in the harmony of heaven . . . May we be led to that glorious life.

Christ, who breathes upon us the Spirit of life, receive our prayers.

TRINITY SUNDAY

Matthew 28:16–20

Let us pray to God, Father, Son and Holy Spirit.

As the mystery of the Holy Trinity has been revealed to the Church, may she continue steadfast in that faith . . . Grant that our differences of order and diversity of worship may find reconciliation in the unity of love and service.

Now let the glory revealed in Jesus Christ fill the whole world with the message of salvation . . . May the voice that proclaimed him at the River Jordan be a voice to bring all nations to his service.

In all our relationships, in all our community, grant us

the mutual love that has no limits and seeks no advantage . . . Be at the heart of our family lives, making them images of the love that is in the Holy Trinity.

We pray for those who suffer from oppression and the inequalities of society . . . Grant them relief and give them perfect freedom in body and mind . . . Have mercy on all who are in error, all who are led astray by false beliefs, and bring them to the true faith.

We give thanks for the departed who now live in continual praise of God, the Three in One . . . In the presence where all mysteries are made known, may they rejoice in his glory.

We offer our prayers in the name of Christ, who lives and reigns with the Father and the Holy Spirit.

PROPER 4

Matthew 7:21–29

For wisdom and constancy in all people, let us pray to the Lord.

Keep the Church firm on the foundation of her Lord and Saviour, that she may hear his words and fulfil the works of faith . . . Let your people not be broken in the time of trial or found wanting in the time of judgement.

Give the strength that comes from you alone to the world where many build on weak foundations, trusting in riches, in position, in their own capacity . . . Grant that those who have the duty of planning for the lives of others may be guided with wisdom and foresight.

As we try to plan our own lives, help us to remember that nothing is secure that does not rest on the foundation of faith . . . Be with those in positions of responsibility in this community, especially those concerned with housing and welfare.

Comfort those who have seen their hopes frustrated, who have built up careers or personal relationships that have fallen into ruin . . . Give them courage for a fresh start in the knowledge of the only sure foundation.

Have mercy on those who have come to judgement trusting in their own words and deeds . . . As they pass through the high waters of death, bring them to safety on the rock of salvation.

May our prayers be accepted through Jesus Christ, the eternal rock of our faith.

PROPER 5

Matthew 9:9–13, 18–26

Let us pray to the Lord who gives life to the Church and to the world.

May the Church, a company of sinners called to repentance, be faithful to her calling and shielded from feeling scorn for those who seem to be outside her fellowship . . . Inspire your ministers to proclaim the message of mercy and healing, and the new life that is open to all who come.

Give light to the world where people exalt themselves and claim their own way of life as the way for all . . . Grant humility and insight to all in authority . . . Bless with integrity those who work in finance.

Bless the parents in this community and bless us in our own families . . . As we care for our children, give us trust in the love of God whose care is greater than any parent . . . Guide the doctors and nurses who work among us.

Have mercy on the sick who have lost hope of being cured. Relieve them in their afflictions with peace of mind and healing of body . . . Comfort the parents who have lost a child or who fear for the life of a child who is sick.

We pray for those who have fallen asleep and have awakened to a new life . . . Whether they were young or old in the years of this world, grant them peaceful rest and resurrection in glory.

May Christ, the good physician, heal our weakness and accept our prayers.

PROPER 6

Matthew 9:35—10:8

Let us pray with confidence to God, who has called us into his service.

As we have been called to be disciples in the Church of God, may we be worthy of our calling . . . Inspire us to proclaim the good news and bring comfort to the needy, seeking no reward but giving thanks for the grace we have received.

Great Shepherd, look with compassion on the peoples of the world who lack purpose and direction . . . Have mercy on those who have been scattered by war or persecution and lead them into the secure fold of your love.

We pray for the spirit of mission, the power to speak of the faith that is in us and to show it in our lives . . . Open our eyes to see where the harvest is ripe in this community . . . Bless those who minister to the needy and the homeless, and those who teach in our schools.

We pray for the sick in mind or body, the outcasts from society and those who are in the power of evil . . . May all who work to heal or to reclaim be given the compassion and the power which led the first disciples to fulfil the command of their Lord.

We pray for those whose harvest has been gathered in and now behold their Shepherd in his glory . . . We give thanks that, free from all that can harm them, they have entered the Kingdom of Heaven.

We pray in the name of Christ who has compassion on his wandering sheep.

PROPER 7

Matthew 10:24–39

As faithful disciples, let us pray to our Lord and Master for the Church and for the world.

Give to the Church grace fearlessly to proclaim the words of life . . . Send your strength to overcome our weakness, so that all Christian people shall be valiant for the truth in the face of scorn and indifference.

We pray that the word of God shall be heard in the dark places where people have not known the power of redeeming love . . . Have mercy on the weak and vulnerable who are precious in your sight and save them when they are oppressed.

Give harmony to our families and to all who live and work in this community . . . Reconcile those who are in dispute and mend the broken relationships, so that human love may be as a light to reveal the love of God.

Have mercy on those who are persecuted for their faith . . . Give them courage in their trials and grace to be constant in their service . . . Pardon and restore those who have been driven by suffering to deny their Master.

We pray for those who took up their cross and followed their Master in this life and have now passed to eternal life with him . . . May the light of heaven shine upon them as they rise in glory.

May Christ our Lord be now and always acknowledged in our prayers.

PROPER 8

Matthew 10:40–42

Let us pray to God, the source of all prophecy and all righteousness.

Give to the Church the gifts that inspired the prophets of old, to warn and to encourage at this time and always . . . Make your people worthy to be prophets of your word and counted as righteous through your grace.

Be with those who in the world speak the words of truth and the message of salvation . . . Open the hearts of the powerful and the humble alike to receive those who come in your name.

Grant us grace to discern the presence of Christ in those we know and in the stranger . . . May we be hospitable and welcoming in our homes . . . May the doors in this community be open to the Lord who comes in many ways.

We pray for those who are suffering from drought, all who are thirsty and must go far to find water . . . Guide and enable those who work for their relief and grant the blessing of good water where it is lacking.

May the faithful departed receive their reward and share in the fountain of living water in heaven . . . Grant that we may be constant in this world and enter at last into the world to come.

May our prayers be accepted in the name of Christ who has called us to be his messengers.

PROPER 9

Matthew 11:16–19, 25–30

Let us pray with confidence to the Father, Lord of heaven and earth.

Bless and strengthen the Church to which the mystery of faith has been revealed . . . Grant that she may speak the words of comfort to all people, to meet their diversity without losing the integrity of truth.

Come with healing into the discontent of the world, to take away the suspicion that separates people and sets them against each other . . . Teach those who think themselves wise in this world to trust the wisdom of the simple.

Make us more gentle and humble in our dealings with others . . . Give us insight to see the burdens that many in our community are bearing, and generosity to bring relief.

Have mercy on those who are bowed down under heavy loads, wearied by poverty and hunger, by sickness or by the weight of unresolved sin . . . Bring them to your side, to find comfort and assurance in your love.

We pray for the departed who have laid down their burdens and found eternal rest . . . We give thanks that to them all mysteries have been revealed and the fullness of the divine love made known.

We offer our prayers in the name of Christ, whose yoke is easy and whose burden is light.

PROPER 10

Matthew 13:1–9, 18–23

Let us pray that the word of God shall be fertile in the Church and in the world.

Give to the Church the grace to receive the word of faith in obedience and to bring forth good fruit for the salvation of many . . . Take away all that hinders her witness, so that all her people may share in her ministry and work for the harvest that is to come.

Come in mercy to all who are hungry for the word but are held back by the cares of living . . . Rouse the indifferent and nurture those who are moving towards the Kingdom but have not yet come to full commitment . . . Bless the servants of your word who are bringing its healing power to the nations.

As we share our lives with others who are close to us, help us to live as those who have heard and received the word, that we may be bearers of good news and doers of good work . . . May this community be as a field which the Lord has blessed.

We pray for all those in many places who are suffering from failed harvests and who struggle to cultivate infertile land ... We pray for people who once believed but have fallen away through trouble and persecution: bring them back to know the richness of your love.

We give thanks for the departed whose harvest has ripened and been gathered in where new life begins ... Give us grace to follow their example as we wait for our time of fruition.

We pray in the name of Christ who brings to us the good seed of the Kingdom.

PROPER 11

Matthew 13:24–30, 36–43

Let us pray that the Church and the world may be preserved from evil.

Shield the Church against all that would damage her witness, from false doctrine, from pride, from indifference to life that seems to lie outside her care ... Give her ministers wisdom to discern between good and evil and to guide their people in the right way.

Root out corruption in the high places of the world, where power is misused and rights are disregarded ... Strengthen and prosper those who work against difficulty to bring a better life for others.

May we seek to see and correct the wrong that is in ourselves and to discern and foster what can be used for good ... Protect this community from all evil that threatens its peace, and let all live together in harmony.

Come in mercy to those whose lives have been blighted by misfortune or false judgement, those whose hopes have been unfulfilled, those whose minds are torn by temptation . . . Bring them back to their place in the good harvest of your love.

Be merciful to your servants who have gone astray in this world and have been called to judgement . . . Restore in them your image that they have marred and grant them a place with those who have kept the faith.

May our prayers be accepted in the name of Christ who has planted us in righteousness.

PROPER 12

Matthew 13:31–33, 44–52

For the growth and purity of the Kingdom, let us pray to the Lord.

Guide your Church to cherish and cultivate the precious seed of the Kingdom, that all your people may be gathered into one in holiness . . . Teach us to recognize the old and the new treasures that have been revealed and entrusted to us, to maintain past integrity and explore new opportunities.

May all that tends to goodness and love in the world be recognized and developed . . . Give to the rulers of the nations and to all in authority the understanding that there is a greater kingdom than their own, and a richer treasure than their wealth, so that life for all shall be more abundant.

Help us to value more fully the gifts that we have received and to help our families, our friends and neighbours, towards the Kingdom . . . Make us wise in our households, to be faithful to the past and open to the future.

Have mercy on those suffering from despair and depression because they have not known the true values that lead to contentment . . . Set free all whose lives are constrained by the errors of the past and those who are afraid of what is new.

Receive into life the souls who have been brought to the eternal shore in the net of salvation and made members of the Kingdom towards which they strove on earth . . . May they find rest, and treasure greater than they have known.

We offer our prayers in the name of Christ, through whom we are members of the Kingdom.

PROPER 13

Matthew 14:13–21

Let us pray to the Lord, the generous giver of all our needs, for the Church and for the world.

Grant that the Church may have grace to feed all who are hungry for the word of salvation . . . Through the divine feeding of the Holy Communion, keep your people faithful in obedience and untiring in works of mercy.

Come to the aid of the multitudes who wander in the wilderness places of the world, unsatisfied but not knowing what they are seeking . . . Give to those in authority hearts of compassion not to turn away those who need their care.

Make us more hospitable in our homes, ready to meet the bodily and emotional needs of those who come into our lives . . . Bless the helpers in this community who feed the hungry and bring food to those who cannot prepare it for themselves.

Have mercy on the hungry, the victims of famine and all who always have too little food for their needs . . . Give power to the agencies that work for their relief.

We pray for all who were sustained in their earthly bodies and now have tasted the fullness of God's bounty . . . We give thanks that they rejoice with the great multitude of the faithful departed.

May our prayers be heard through the compassion of Christ.

PROPER 14

Matthew 14:22–33

Let us pray that God will uphold and guide the Church and bless the world.

Grant that the Church may hear the call of her Lord and come to him in trust . . . May all Christian people keep their eyes fixed on him, knowing that they can do nothing without him but in his power can do great things.

Correct those who, in the pride of authority, trust too much in their own strength . . . Give courage to the many in the world who are oppressed by fear of what seems to them strange or unknown.

When our daily work is hard, when our relationships become difficult, teach us to know where we must look for help . . . May we see Christ in the life around us and recognize him when he comes in unfamiliar and unexpected ways.

Have mercy on those who are battered by the strains of life and feel they are making no progress towards better things . . . Pardon and rescue all who have been drawn into forbidden occult ways and can no longer see their true God.

We give thanks for the departed, called by Christ to come to him . . . May those who have crossed the stormy sea of life feel the touch of his hand and find rest.

We pray in the name of Christ who takes away our fear.

PROPER 15

Matthew 15:10–28

For the many peoples of the Church and in the world, let us pray to the Lord.

Make the Church open to the needs of all who come, never forgetting that the good news of salvation is for all people . . . Give to your ministers grace to help those who come in need, and to feed them with the bread of life.

Heal the wounds of suspicion that divide nations and races . . . Give to those in authority compassion to hear the cry of those who come to seek help in their distress and not to send them away without relief.

Make us more alert to the needs that are around us, more willing to share the great benefits that we have received in body, mind and spirit . . . Bless the families in this community and bring hope to those who are in trouble.

We pray for all sick children, for their parents and for those who work for their care and healing . . . We remember especially those who have been ill for a long time, that they may be brought to a full and happy life.

We give thanks for the departed who, having trusted in you for healing and sustenance in this world, have entered into the fullness of joy . . . May we follow them in the faith that does not falter until all is revealed.

We pray in the name of Christ who heals and feeds all who call upon his mercy.

PROPER 16

Matthew 16:13–20

Let us pray to God who sent his Son to be the Saviour of the world.

Grant that the Church, mindful of the privilege of her foundation and the duty of her commission, shall ever confess the faith of Christ as Son of God, the only Redeemer . . . Strengthen her members firmly in that faith, to keep it whole and pure from generation to generation.

Have mercy on those who are living in error and uncertainty, who wander in the world without finding the truth of God . . . Give to those in authority the wisdom to know that their power comes from him alone . . . May they fulfil their duty on the firm foundation of justice and truth.

In all our lives with others, in our families and in our places of work, help us to show ourselves as members of the Kingdom . . . Give us grace to acknowledge the Messiah in all we do, and to lead others to trust in him.

May the sick and afflicted, the lonely, the homeless, and those who are near to death, receive comfort and hope in the Lord who desires to give them the peace and assurance of his Kingdom . . . Bless all who seek to relieve suffering: keep them patient and constant in their work.

We give thanks for those to whom the gates of the Kingdom of Heaven have been opened and who now rejoice with the faithful from blessed Peter to this time ... Keep us firm in faith until we share with them in that eternal Kingdom.

May our prayers be accepted in the name of Christ, the Son of the living God.

PROPER 17

Matthew 16:21–28

For the suffering in the Church and in the world, let us pray to the Lord.

Give grace to the Church to show forth the death of our Lord, to follow where he leads and proclaim his salvation ... Give courage and strength to all ministers of the gospel when their burdens are heavy.

Forgive the greed for material wealth that damages many lives in the world ... Have pity on all who are in misery through their own selfishness or by the indifference of those who rule them ... Bring them into the way of service and salvation.

In our daily pilgrimage may we bear with gladness both the troubles that come to us and the little things which tempt us to impatience ... As we see Christ in all things, may we bring his light to all whose way through this world is joined with ours.

Have mercy on those who bear the heavy crosses of sickness or poverty, of loneliness or bereavement ...

Bless and relieve all who suffer contempt and persecution for the faith they profess.

We pray for those who having laid aside their burdens have seen the Son of Man in his glory as Son of God and are with him for ever . . . Give us grace so to follow his Cross in this world that we may at last enter into eternal life.

We pray in the name of Christ who has borne our sins and our sorrows.

PROPER 18

Matthew 18:15–20

For the spirit of peace in the Church and in the world, let us pray to the Lord.

Give to the Church perfect harmony among all her members, and let her witness never be hindered by the scandal of dissension . . . As we come together for worship, may our hearts be so filled with love for one another that we shall be as lights to the world.

Bring agreement between nations which are in dispute and distrust . . . Heal the anger of litigation and give a new spirit to those who profit from the disagreements of others.

If there is tension in our families, with our neighbours or with any we know, give us grace to confess our faults and to seek reconciliation . . . Bring harmony to all in this community who are held apart by anger and resentment.

Bless and relieve all who have been ruined by litigation or broken by disputes that have turned to bitterness . . .

Restore those who suffer inwardly from their refusal to be reconciled . . . Have mercy on all in prison, granting them acknowledgement of faults and new hope for the future.

We pray for those who were gathered together in the name of the Lord when they were in this world, and are gathered into the great company of the blessed in heaven . . . May the peace they now enjoy rest upon all who are still on their way.

We pray that our prayers may be accepted in Christ, in whose name we are gathered together.

PROPER 19

Matthew 18:21–35

That all may do to others as they would have done to them, let us pray to the Lord.

Give to the Church grace to speak the word of pardon and to show its power by her example . . . Let all who confess the faith of Christ acknowledge the mercy they have received and in all things be slow to find fault in others, quick to forgive offences.

Have compassion on the nations which suffer under heavy loads of debt . . . Bring a new spirit of generosity to those who have much, that they may be moved to relieve those who have little . . . May those who hold authority exercise it with mercy.

Guide us to be merciful to those who need our mercy . . . In all our relationships, may we be the first to forgive and make peace . . . Bring the spirit of love to solve the disputes and demands which are in this community.

We pray for those who bear a heavy burden of personal debt and find no way of escape . . . Guide those who seek to help them in their problems . . . Have mercy on all who are imprisoned for debt, and on their families.

We give thanks for the departed whose debts of sin committed in this world have been forgiven and who have entered into life where anger and fear have ceased . . . We pray that we in our time may receive the same mercy.

We offer our prayers through Christ who has cancelled our debt of sin.

PROPER 20

Matthew 20:1–16

For the mercy and the justice of the Kingdom, let us pray to the Lord.

Give to all Christian people the grace to be faithful labourers in your service . . . Desiring no reward but the knowledge of doing your will, may the whole Church be diligent in working for peace on earth and for the coming of the Kingdom.

May there be justice wherever people deal with one another as employers or employed . . . Bring harmony and mutual trust into all labour relations, so that goodwill shall prevail and the common good be accomplished.

Keep us cheerful in our daily tasks, honourable in duty and with regard for those with whom we work . . . May all who work in this community be recognized and respected for what they do.

Strengthen and relieve those who labour long and hard, who work in bad conditions or for low wages . . . Pardon those who exploit their workers, and turn their hearts . . . Have mercy on all who have been long without work, and grant them the opportunities they desire.

We pray for those who have come to the end of their toil and entered into rest . . . May we at last be called with them to the life where all are equal in joy and receive their reward in the nearer presence of God.

We pray in the name of Christ, the loving master of all who labour.

PROPER 21

Matthew 21:23–32

Let us pray that the will of God shall be obeyed in the Church and in the world.

Grant that the members of the Church, knowing the source of all power and enabling true authority, may humbly obey and cheerfully serve in their various callings . . . Keep us faithful in work and worship, that God's will may be done.

Look with pity upon the world where stubborn hearts turn away from truth and refuse its challenge . . . May there be integrity in keeping promises and agreements wherever they are made, between nations or between individuals.

Keep us faithful in our promises and honest in our dealings . . . Give us grace to spread the word of God to our families, our friends and neighbours, and those with whom we work.

Have compassion on all who feel betrayed by those they have trusted . . . Keep them from resentment and help them to heal their relationships . . . Come to those who know that they have failed in love and duty, and show them the way of return.

We pray for the departed who have passed through this world, sometimes in obedience and sometimes in rebellion . . . With all offences pardoned, may they enter into the joy of the Lord who first called them to his service.

That our prayers may be the prayers of faithful children, we offer them in the name of Christ the Son of God.

PROPER 22

Matthew 21:33–46

Let us pray that the Church and the world shall be conformed to the sovereignty of God.

Grant that the Church may reveal the loving power of God in her works and in her worship . . . As we seek to use rightly the gifts we have received, teach us to honour those in every generation who make known his commands.

Give wisdom to all in authority not to seek for more power than has been entrusted to them . . . May all who have control of this world's goods be just and faithful in their dealings.

Bless us with the grace to tell our families and friends and all our acquaintance that all good things come from God and to show that faith in our lives . . . May this community be blessed with justice and compassion in all that affects the welfare of its members.

Have mercy on those who suffer for speaking the words of truth and claiming for God the honour and obedience that are his due . . . Bring relief to all who suffer because what they need for their sustenance has been unjustly withheld.

We pray for all who after being ignored and rejected in this world have entered into glory . . . May they rejoice in the good fruit of eternal life.

We pray in the name of Christ, the cornerstone of our faith.

PROPER 23

Matthew 22:11–14

Let us pray for a gracious response to the love of God in the Church and in the world.

May the Church ever give glory to God for his grace and the great benefits of his love . . . Let all Christian people hear his call and respond gladly and without reservation.

We pray for a world where many reject the true wealth of faithful obedience for the false wealth of material things . . . Grant that those who control its resources shall be gracious to the needs of all people.

Bless those in this community who care for the poor and helpless, find shelter for the homeless and minister to the sick . . . Make us more grateful for all that we have received and more willing to share it with others.

We pray for all who have been hurt by the rejection of their love, whose happy relationships have been broken, or who have lost by folly and selfishness what they once enjoyed . . . Comfort the lonely and those who have forgotten their self-respect, and show them that they are loved and accepted for themselves.

We give thanks for those who have gone from this world to be guests at the great marriage feast of heaven . . . May they be cleansed from all their sins and clothed with a garment of worthiness that by their own works they could never gain.

May our prayers be accepted in the name of Christ, who calls us to sit at his table and be his guests.

PROPER 24

Matthew 22:15–22

For peace and harmony in the Church and in the world let us pray to the Lord.

Grant that the Church shall always bear witness to God as supreme, rendering the honour and worship that are his due . . . May all Christian people show forth their faith by their words and by their deeds.

We pray for justice and honest dealing between nations and between individuals . . . Give to those in authority the wisdom to know the limits of their power and to demand no more than is right.

Bless us, our families, neighbours and friends, with obedience in all things lawful and courage to resist injustice . . . Bless those who manage the finances of this community and give them right judgement in all their decisions.

Have mercy on all who bear heavy burdens of taxation for the benefit of the few and not for the common good . . . Guide and strengthen those whose Christian allegiance is divided and uncertain, and keep them in the way of truth.

We give thanks for the departed who have rendered their duty in this world and gone to their rest . . . Give them peace in the realm where nothing can challenge their whole loyalty to their God and Saviour.

May Christ guide us in all our decisions and accept our prayers which we offer in his name.

PROPER 25

Matthew 22:34–46

Let us pray that the commandments of God shall be obeyed at all times and in all places.

Grant to the members of the Church unreserved love for God and unselfish love for all people . . . May the glory of Christ be proclaimed as we seek to fulfil the great law of love.

Send a new spirit of love into the disputes between nations and races . . . Where there is suspicion bring trust, where there is anger bring compassion . . . Give peace in all places of war and violence.

In all we do and say, in our lives with families, friends and neighbours, let us show the love which is demanded from those who claim to love God . . . May the Lord of all love rule in our hearts.

Have mercy on those who are torn by anger and bitterness, who have never known love or have lost the way of loving . . . Restore their peace and bring them new hope.

We pray for the departed, for those who loved deeply in this world and for those who failed in love . . . May they be received together into the love that is everlasting.

We pray through Christ in whom the Law and the Prophets are fulfilled.

or BIBLE SUNDAY

Matthew 24:30–35

Let us pray that the word of God shall be heard and honoured by all.

Keep the Church faithful to the revelation made known in Scripture . . . Bless all who preach and make them worthy messengers of the good news . . . Grant that all Christian people shall hear and receive the word with reverence.

Give to those in authority the grace to know that their power will not last for ever and to use it for the good of others . . . Teach all people so to read the signs of the present time that there shall be wise planning for the future . . . Bless individuals and societies who work for the distribution of bibles throughout the world.

Help us in the duty of bible reading and study, to grow daily in obedience to its word . . . Bless all in this community who are spreading the faith by teaching and example.

Pardon all who have lost the faith they once had and no longer seek to know God's word . . . Bring them back to

the true path where their lives will find meaning . . .
Have mercy on all who are persecuted for their
Christian teaching.

We pray for those who have come to the end of their
time on earth and seen the glory of the Son of Man . . .
May they be joyful in the eternal life which is the
promise of Scripture.

We pray in the name of Christ, the Word whose words
lead us to salvation.

DEDICATION FESTIVAL

Matthew 21:12–16

Let us pray that the holiness of God shall be acknowledged in the Church and in the world.

Give to the Church due reverence for her places of
worship that they may truly be houses of prayer . . . Let
them be open and welcoming to all who enter, but
never marred by what is unfitting to their dedication.

In all trade and commerce may the holiness of God, the
provider of all, be remembered . . . Let there be honesty
in all dealings and respect for those who come as
pilgrims and seekers to holy places.

Help us through our own behaviour to show to our
families, friends and neighbours the reverence that we
have for this place of worship . . . May it be a beacon of
hope and a centre of peace for all in our community.

As the blind and the lame were healed in the Temple,
so may the healing power of God come to all who are
afflicted in body or mind and make them whole . . .
Bless all who offer the ministry of healing in churches
and homes.

Receive the souls of the departed who need no earthly temple as they share in the eternal praise of heaven . . . Give us such reverence in our worship that we too may come to that glory.

May our prayers be accepted and our worship cleansed in the name of Christ.

FOURTH SUNDAY BEFORE ADVENT

Matthew 24:1–14

Let us pray for the faith of the Church and the peace of the world.

Grant to the Church the grace to be steadfast and endure in all difficulties, to avoid false doctrine and to keep uncorrupted the faith entrusted to her . . . Make her a strong defence for all people in times of trouble.

Bring an end to the warfare and strife that mar the harmony of the world . . . Turn aside the abuse of power and save your people from the leaders whose selfish aims are leading to disaster . . . Bring greater concern for the preservation of all that has been wonderfully created.

Give us constancy in faith when we feel under pressure, and make us a source of comfort for those whose lives touch our own . . . Bring a happy resolution to any disputes that damage the life of this community.

We pray for all who are suffering from natural disasters, for the victims of war and human cruelty . . . Comfort those who are persecuted for their faith and those who have been betrayed by people they have trusted.

Receive the souls of the departed who have endured

affliction and temptation and come to their rest . . .
Freed from all the perils of this life, may they know the
perfect peace of heaven.

We pray in the name of Christ, the only Saviour.

ALL SAINTS' SUNDAY

Matthew 5:1–12

Let us pray for the blessings of God on the Church and
the world.

Grant that the Church, strengthened by the witness of
the saints through all ages, may bear faithful witness to
the message of the gospel . . . May all Christian people,
called to be saints in their own time, be worthy of those
who have gone before and kept the faith.

May all who work for peace in the world be blessed in
their endeavour . . . May the meek and humble by their
example move the rich and powerful to be compassionate and seek the common good.

Make our lives more worthy of the blessings promised
to those who follow the way of the Lord . . . May we be
loving and peaceable in all our relationships and may
our families and friends be led into holiness, and our
whole community be blessed.

Have mercy on those who are persecuted for the sake
of their faith, on all who are slandered and falsely
accused . . . Give them strength, and change the hearts
of those who oppress them . . . Satisfy those who
hunger for the good food of righteousness, and relieve
those whose lives are constrained by the hunger of the
body.

We give thanks for the departed who have run their

course and are numbered with the saints in everlasting glory . . . May we so live our lives that we too shall be received into their fellowship.

May Christ, the Lord, the example and the support of all the saints, receive our prayers.

THIRD SUNDAY BEFORE ADVENT

Matthew 25:1–13

That we and all people may be always ready in service, let us pray to the Lord.

By grace may the lamp of faith be for ever burning brightly in the Church . . . Keep all Christian people alert for the coming of the Lord and fit to enter into his presence.

We pray for a more equal distribution of the goods of this world . . . We pray that ignorance may be dispelled by sound teaching and that folly may yield to wisdom, so that all may share in the heritage of creation.

Help us to be provident and generous in our use of money and in all our dealings with others . . . May the spirit of true charity prevail in our families and in all this community.

Look with mercy on all who are grieving for lost opportunities, and bring new hope into their lives . . . Bring aid to the homeless and to all who feel themselves rejected by society.

We pray for the departed who have been called into the presence of the Lord and share with him the heavenly feast . . . We pray that we in our time may rejoice in the company of the blessed.

May our prayers be accepted through Christ, the divine Bridegroom.

SECOND SUNDAY BEFORE ADVENT

Matthew 25:14–30

Let us pray that the gifts of God may be rightly used.

Bless the Church with generosity and care for all . . . Give grace to your people so to use all that has been entrusted to them that they may bring new hope to many and show forth the glory of God.

Bring to a world where dealing is often hard and competitive the spirit of compassion, so that those who gain much may share more generously . . . Give wisdom to the rich to know that all wealth is the gift of God.

Help us to value more gratefully the gifts we have been given, to develop and to use them for the good of others . . . Guide with wisdom those who are responsible for the finances of this community.

Have mercy on the poor who have nothing they can develop to ease their burden, and guide them to ways where they may find relief . . . Raise up from despair those who know they have not fulfilled what they might have done, and open to them again the way they have lost.

We pray for those who have completed their task in this world and have entered into the joy of their Master . . . May they rest in the peace promised to his faithful servants.

We pray as the servants of Christ from whom all good things come.

CHRIST THE KING

Matthew 25:31–46

For the spirit of love and service, let us pray to the Lord.

Grant to the Church light to know the will of God and grace to perform it . . . Make all Christian people true followers of Christ in their lives day by day.

Fill the world with the spirit of compassion, that the powerful may use their power to help the weak . . . Break through the barriers that divide people and nations, and draw all together for the common good.

Give us deeper compassion, open our eyes to see the presence of Christ in all people . . . Grant us insight to know where we can give help in the needs of friends and neighbours and in all our community, and grace to offer it.

We pray for all who suffer, for the poor and hungry, for the sick and the homeless, for prisoners and those who have no one to care for them . . . Bring them relief in their misery and strengthen all who as individuals or organizations work for relief.

Have mercy on those who have passed from this world and come to judgement . . . Pardon their failures and receive them in the compassion of Christ . . . Grant mercy to us all when we are called to account at the end of our lives.

May our prayers be accepted in the name of Christ, our Judge and our Redeemer.

Principal Service

Year B

FIRST SUNDAY OF ADVENT

Mark 13:24–37

As we prepare for the coming of the Lord, let us pray for the Church and for the world.

Grant that the whole Church, as a faithful servant, shall be vigilant to know and diligent to perform the will of her Master . . . In watching and in penitence, may your people make ready for the coming joy of the Nativity.

Guide all in authority, to discern the signs and to act with wisdom and justice . . . Open their minds and direct their wills to look beyond the immediate advantage to the lasting good of all humanity.

At this Advent time give us grace to serve by example and by deeds those who are close to us, our families, friends and neighbours and those with whom we work . . . As we look towards the season of Christmas, may we remember with humility and gratitude the great love of the Father in sending the Son.

Have mercy on all who are suffering from natural disasters, and relieve their distress . . . Come to those who are in darkness and lead them to recognize the signs by which their lives can be guided.

We pray for those who have known the coming of the Lord at the end of their lives . . . May they rest in the peace to which he has called them, and may we be ready for our calling, and receive mercy.

We pray in the name of Christ, whose words will never pass away.

SECOND SUNDAY OF ADVENT

Mark 1:1–8

In the confidence of the gospel, let us pray to the Lord.

Let the Church give thanks and praise for the good news of salvation, and receive the power to proclaim it to the world . . . May all Christian people prepare in humility and love to celebrate the coming of Christ.

Grant to the whole world the knowledge of the divine mercy revealed in Jesus Christ, that all people may come though repentance to new life . . . Make straight the crooked ways of the world and give light to the dark places.

Give us grace to be messengers of the good news to those whose lives come near to our own . . . Send the healing power of the Holy Spirit to guide all in our community into the way of peace.

Have mercy on all who are held in the power of unrepented sin, and lead them back into the right way . . . Strengthen those who suffer indifference and hostility as they preach the word of God.

We give thanks for those who in this world received the word of salvation, showed its power in their lives and are now at rest . . . Keep us faithful in the way where they have gone before, until we come to the Kingdom.

May our prayers be accepted through Christ by whom we are baptized in the Holy Spirit.

THIRD SUNDAY OF ADVENT

John 1:6–8, 19–28

For light to know and to follow the truth, let us pray to
the Lord.

Make the Church a powerful witness to the light that
has come into the world . . . Through the preaching of
the word, and through the water of baptism, may
God's people be gathered into one body.

Grant that the messengers of God may be heard
throughout the world . . . Where material wealth and
comfort abound in a spiritual wilderness, bring the
light which reveals the true joy of living.

Make us messengers of the Gospel in our daily lives,
and give strength to all in our community who labour
to make known the mighty works of God.

Have mercy on all who suffer in body, mind or spirit
. . . Let the light of hope shine through their darkness
and give them comfort in their affliction.

We give thanks for the departed who were cleansed by
the water of baptism and have passed over the great
water to eternal life . . . May they rest in peace and may
light perpetual shine upon them.

We offer our prayers in the name of Christ, the one
Messiah.

FOURTH SUNDAY OF ADVENT

Luke 1:26–38

Let us pray for grace to prepare for the coming of the Lord.

Fill the Church with the power of the Holy Spirit announced to the Virgin Mary . . . May the faith of her response be granted to all Christian people . . . May they be open to hear and obey the calling of God.

Draw the nations of the world into the Kingdom of the Messiah, that those who hold authority may use it for the good of all . . . May the divine power overshadow the places of strife and violence, and bring them peace.

Bless us, our families, friends and neighbours as we make ready for the holy time of Christmas . . . Bless especially all the families in this community who are expecting the birth of a child and bring them the joy of a new life.

Have mercy on all who are perplexed and troubled, uncertain where their lives are leading ℘. Give them assurance that God, to whom all things are possible, is very close to them in their need.

We pray for the departed who heard and tried to follow the command of God in this world and have now come to fullness of life in him . ℘ We rejoice that they praise him with the Blessed Virgin Mary and all the saints.

We pray in the name of Christ, the Son of the Most High.

CHRISTMAS DAY

As for Year A, p. 5.

FIRST SUNDAY OF CHRISTMAS

Luke 2:15–21

Let us pray for the Church and for the world, glorifying and praising God.

Bless the worship of the Church, that it may be filled with reverence for this holy birth . . . Teach your faithful people to treasure the message of salvation and to ponder it in their hearts.

Give peace to the world, peace between nations and races, peace where people are in dispute . . . May the love of the Holy Family of Bethlehem draw all into the way that leads to eternal life.

Grant us the light of faith given to the shepherds, that we may make known the wonder of the Nativity . . . As we rejoice at this time with our families and friends, make us truly grateful for the wonderful gift of the Holy Child.

Have mercy on all who are sad and lonely at this time, the sick and injured, the bereaved and those who are near to death . . . May the name of Jesus be their strength.

We pray for those who in this world gave thanks for the birth of their Lord and have passed through death to be born to eternal life in him . . . May our worship this day be joined with theirs.

We offer our prayers through Christ, given the name of Jesus in his humanity.

SECOND SUNDAY OF CHRISTMAS

As for Year A, p. 7.

THE EPIPHANY

As for Year A, p. 8.

THE BAPTISM OF CHRIST (FIRST SUNDAY OF EPIPHANY)

Mark 1:4–11

For the cleansing of the Church and of the world, let us pray to the Lord.

Keep the Church true in obedience to the example and command of her Lord to baptize for the forgiveness of sins and into the life of faith . . . Give grace to all Christian people to live according to the promises made at their baptism.

We pray that the whole world may know the healing power of God . . . Let the voice of his messengers be heard and his name be praised among all nations.

We pray for those who at this time are preparing for baptism, remembering especially those known to us and those who live in this community . . . We pray that godparents shall remember their responsibility for the spiritual life of those they have sponsored.

Have mercy on all who have fallen away from their vows of baptism or other solemn promises that they have made . . . Grant them the guidance of the Holy Spirit to bring them back into the way of holiness.

We pray for the departed who began their earthly lives

by following Christ in baptism and have passed with
him through death to life . . . May their joy be for ever in
the worship of the Holy Trinity.

We pray in the name of Christ who has made us his
own in baptism.

SECOND SUNDAY OF EPIPHANY

John 1:43–51

Let us pray for obedience to the call of God in all things.

As the first disciples came to faith in Christ, so may the
Church be faithful in following him . . . May she be
made worthy to know and to reveal the mystery of
salvation.

Where there is hostility between nations and races,
where a name can arouse suspicion, bring the peace of
Christ . . . Teach all people to trust one another and find
friendship for each in seeking the good of all.

Help us all to guide in the right way those who are near
to us . . . Let the homes of this community be blessed
with the presence of the Lord.

Have mercy on all who are imprisoned in old feuds and
rivalries, who have ceased to believe in the power of
good . . . Grant that they may lose their fear, and see
love in the eyes of the stranger.

We give thanks for the departed to whom heaven has
been opened and the divine vision granted . . . May our
faith in this world bring us to follow Christ until we
come to eternal life.

We pray in the name of Christ, the Son of God, the King
of Israel.

THIRD SUNDAY OF EPIPHANY

John 2:1–11

Let us pray to God, the giver of all good things to the Church and to the world.

Grant that the Church may so obey the commands of God that she may be strengthened by the good wine of his love . . . May we find the mystery of grace in the life of every day.

We pray for the needs of the world, for fellowship and mutual care in sorrow and in joy . . . Have compassion on those who have not enough for their needs, and guide those who are able to bring relief.

We ask for your blessing on our families . . . Bless all who are recently married or soon to be married . . . Give them joy at their weddings and constancy in their love.

We pray for the broken marriages and the families where bitterness has driven out love . . . Revive in them the first vision of their joy and restore their love in the unbounded love of Christ.

Receive the souls of those who have passed through the pleasures and troubles of this world and found the good wine at last . . . May they rejoice in the great wedding feast of heaven.

We offer our prayers in the name of Christ who gives abundantly to all who bring their need to him.

FOURTH SUNDAY OF EPIPHANY

Mark 1:21–28

For deliverance from evil, let us pray to the Lord.

Grant to the Church the grace to resist evil and to bring

release to those who are in its power . . . In the authority of the Lord, may she do his present work on earth.

We pray for the healing of the nations from all strife and violence . . . May those in authority, made free from greed and the love of power, rule with justice and mercy . . . May the darkness be dispersed and the glory of God revealed.

Be close to us, with our families and friends and in all our relationships . . . Keep them free from all that would harm them . . . Forgive the faults and imperfections in this community and fill it with your good Spirit.

Have mercy on the mentally ill and give patience to those who care for them . . . We pray that all who through folly or intention have fallen into evil ways shall be made whole.

We pray for those who have died unreconciled and in fear . . . Grant them the peace that here they did not know and the vision that they have lost.

We offer our prayers in the name of Christ, the name which casts out all evil.

THE PRESENTATION OF CHRIST

As for Year A, p. 13.

EPIPHANY 5 (PROPER 1)

Mark 1:29–39

Let us pray for the healing of all ills in the Church and in the world.

May the Church ever proclaim the message of salvation

and bring to others the new life which is in Christ
. . . May she receive in love all who come to her with
their needs.

We pray for all who are worn down by the weight of
responsibility, those who are under stress in their work
and their relationships . . . Give them the wisdom to
draw apart, the grace to be still and find new strength
in the presence of God.

Bless us in our families, and with our friends and
neighbours, to care for the sick and help the weak . . .
May our homes be open and welcoming.

Have compassion on those who are suffering from illness or injury, bring them relief and give skill to all who
work for healing . . . Comfort and uphold those who
care for the sick in their own homes.

We give thanks for the departed who are free from pain
and weakness and are made whole in the life of heaven
. . . May we in our time be granted the same mercy.

We pray in the name of Christ, the divine Healer.

EPIPHANY 6 (PROPER 2)

Mark 1:40–45

For the cleansing of all that is unclean in the Church
and in the world, let us pray to the Lord.

Give to all Christian people the wisdom that discerns
when to speak out and when to be silent; when to be
active and when to be still . . . Fill us with the divine
compassion which offers healing and salvation.

Have mercy on the outcasts of the world, the refugees
and the homeless, those who are shunned for their race
or their faith . . . Change the hearts of the oppressors

and persecutors, that all people may value one another as children of God.

Give grace to us, our families and friends, to hear the calls of distress and seek to help . . . Guide the members of our community who work for the relief of those in need.

We pray for the sick, especially those whose affliction makes them shunned and despised . . . We pray for doctors and nurses working with difficult and pro- longed cases.

Receive in mercy the souls of the departed, that healed from all the pain and trouble of this world, and cleansed from all their sins, they may rejoice in the company of the saints and the presence of the Lord . . . Grant to us at our end the blessing of eternal life.

May our prayers be accepted in the name of Christ whose compassion never fails.

EPIPHANY 7 (PROPER 3)

Mark 2:1–12

Let us pray for the mercy of God, to pardon and to heal all ills in the Church and in the world.

May the Church be always open to those who come . . . Cleanse her from the pride of claiming sole possession of the power of God . . . May her ministers be compas- sionate to both spiritual and physical needs, that the glory of God may be seen in all his works.

We pray for all who work to relieve suffering, who set aside their own interest for the benefit of others . . . When the problems of the world seem beyond remedy, open new ways through which people may be made whole.

Grant to us concern for sickness and distress, and give us the will to help those around us who are in need . . . May our community be filled with the spirit of friendship and mutual help.

We pray for the sick, for the disabled and all who cannot help themselves . . . Bless with skill and compassion those who care for them . . . Give them faith in the power of God to heal when human hope fails.

Have mercy on the departed who have come through the winding ways of this world, to be brought at last to the feet of Christ . . . Their infirmities healed and their sins forgiven, may they glorify God in eternal life.

May our prayers be accepted through Christ, who forgives the sins of the world.

SECOND SUNDAY BEFORE LENT

John 1:1–14

For the new life that is in Christ, let us pray to the Lord.

Make the Church a true witness to the light that has come into the world . . . Grant to all Christian people so to be faithful to Christ that as he shared our humanity we may be drawn into his divinity.

May the Lord by whom all things were made look with compassion on the world . . . May the people who know him bring his light to others and those who know him not receive that light.

As the Word was made flesh for our salvation, may he dwell among us, be close to us in our families and friendships and with our neighbours . . . Give us grace to behold his glory in our lives day by day.

Have mercy on those who are in the darkness of suffering, the sick, the bereaved, the oppressed, the homeless . . . Bring them relief in their need through the light that darkness cannot contain.

We pray for the departed who have walked in the light through this world and have come to the perfect light of heaven . . . May we with them become the children of God for ever.

We pray in the name of Christ, the true Light, the eternal Word.

SUNDAY BEFORE LENT

Mark 9:2–9

Let us pray that the Church and the world shall be filled with the glory of God.

Guide the Church to be faithful to the wisdom of the past and open to the revelation of the future . . . As we rejoice in our times of worship, keep us from lingering too long on the heights, and lead us back to do the work appointed for us.

Grant to all the peoples of the world the blessing of quiet times set apart from daily concerns, and renewal of strength for the service of all . . . May those who hold authority find the inner peace that will lead them to seek the peace of the nations.

May our lives be so filled with the glory of the Lord, that we may show his grace in our lives . . . Bless our homes, bless all those whose lives are near to ours, with the wonder which the disciples knew on the holy mountain.

We pray for all who suffer and feel far from the divine love . . . Bring into their lives the radiance of hope and courage to look beyond the present and trust in the promise of a happier time to come.

Receive in mercy those who have walked through the valleys of the world, glimpsed the wonder of the mountains, and are now for ever with Christ . . . Make them perfect in the light which they knew in part and followed with faith.

We pray in the name of Christ, seen in flesh, revealed in glory.

ASH WEDNESDAY

As Year A, p. 20.

FIRST SUNDAY OF LENT

Mark 1:9–15

For resistance to temptation and obedience of life, let us pray to the Lord.

May God's people, baptized in the name of the Holy Trinity, hold fast to the faith they have professed . . . Keep the Church safe in purity of doctrine and holiness of life . . . May the Holy Spirit come down in power to be her guide and lead her away from temptation.

We ask that the divine love may be victorious over all evil in the world . . . Where human authority leads people astray and power is wrongly used, may the power of Christ drive away temptation and cleanse the nations with the sacred water of his baptism.

As the Father rejoiced in the work of the Incarnate Son, may we receive grace to live as those who are pleasing to him in our own time . . . Bless this community, its homes and its places of work with the protection of the divine love.

Have mercy on those who are in the wilderness places of this world, assailed by the wild beasts of doubt and temptation . . . Bring them safely through their trouble, feed those who are hungry in their bodies or in their minds and lead them into the way where they may know and embrace your love.

Give rest to all who have passed through the temptations of this life and now are free from all its dangers . . . Let their praise be joined with the song of the angels who ministered to the Incarnate Lord and now adore him in his glory.

May these our prayers be acceptable in the name of Jesus Christ, the Son, the Beloved.

SECOND SUNDAY OF LENT

Mark 8:31–38

Let us pray to God for right judgement and constancy in faith.

Strengthen the Church to follow the way of the Cross and not to judge in the haste of the moment . . . Help all your faithful people to understand that to save is to lose and to lose is to find, that to give all is to gain all in the power of the risen Christ.

May those who value only the pleasure and satisfaction of the moment learn where true blessedness lies . . . May those who hold power so set their minds on the things that are divine that they may rule with mercy in the things that are human.

Give to us, to our families and friends and neighbours, grace to follow as we are led and wisdom to know what is right in our way of life and what is a hindrance to our faith . . . Strengthen us to let go of the old when you are calling to the new, knowing that in your will there is life and not loss.

Have mercy on those whose burdens in this world are heavy . . . Be near to those who suffer for the sake of the gospel, who have offered their lives for its sake . . . Shield them from harm and bring them to eternal life.

We pray for the departed, those who took up their crosses and carried them to the end of the way and have laid them down in the repose of heaven . . . May we in our time be faithful until we come to share in their joy.

May our prayers be acceptable in Christ who suffered and died for us.

THIRD SUNDAY OF LENT

John 2:13–22

For true holiness in the Church and in the world, let us pray to the Lord.

Shield the Church from all that would corrupt her witness and make her unworthy of her Master . . . May her places of worship be holy and her ministry unblemished by desire for material gain and worldly success.

Have mercy on the world where profit too often stands before people and the love of money is a stronger motive than the love of holiness . . . Drive out the false values by which some grow rich and many are poor, until the whole earth becomes a temple fit for the Lord.

Bless us, our families and friends, with such reverence in our faith that we may value the holiness that is in other people . . . Grant to those who conduct their business in this community the spirit of fair dealing and mutual respect.

Have mercy on all who have suffered loss from the dishonesty of those they trusted . . . Release from evil those who have made material profit their goal and have lost the peace of contentment.

We pray for the departed who having worshipped in this world have died with Christ and been raised up with him . . . May they rejoice in the heavenly Temple where he is the eternal light.

We pray in the name of Christ who drives out all that is evil.

FOURTH SUNDAY OF LENT

John 3:14–21

Let us pray to God for the Church and for the world, giving thanks for the gift of his Son.

May the Church be filled with the light of faith and proclaim the message of salvation . . . Strengthen her ministers to serve the Son of God in word and sacrament so that his glory may be lifted up in the sight of all.

We pray for peace among nations, for light to shine in the dark places of strife and violence and reveal to those who are in conflict their shared humanity . . . May God's love for the world be honoured by the people of the world now and in time to come.

As we praise God for the love that sent his Son, we pray that we may have that love for those with whom we share our lives . . . Give light to direct all that we do together and all the work of this community.

Have mercy on those who have loved darkness rather than light and have fallen into the grip of evil . . . Release them by the love of the Son, raised on the Cross for sinners and raised from death that they might have life.

We pray for the departed who have lived their lives in faith and at the last have not perished but come to eternal life . . . Grant to us to follow their example and share with them the fruit of the same promise.

May our prayers be accepted through Christ, the Saviour of the world.

or MOTHERING SUNDAY

As Year A, p. 25.

FIFTH SUNDAY OF LENT

John 12:20–33

Let us pray that Christ shall be glorified in the Church and in the world.

Grant to your servant Church the zeal to bring all people to Christ and to make known his saving

sacrifice of himself . . . Give her power to drive out evil
and to find her life in his death and resurrection.

Bless all who work to spread the gospel and offer their
lives in its service . . . Guide the seekers after truth, and
lead into the right way those who care only for the
pleasures of this world and the satisfaction of their own
lives.

Jesus said, "Whoever serves me must follow me" —
Make us willing servants of the faith, helping those
around us to find their way and be renewed in the
power of Christ . . . By the power of the Cross may all
divisions in our community be mended, and all hurts
healed.

Have mercy on all who suffer in body, mind or spirit
. . . May they hear the divine voice of power and comfort, be relieved from their affliction and find new life
after loss.

We pray for those who have died to this world . . . May
they grow into the life of heaven where joy is endless
and what has been offered on earth comes to perfect
fruition.

We pray in the name of Christ, lifted on the Cross for
our salvation.

PALM SUNDAY

As Year A, p. 27.

MAUNDY THURSDAY

As Year A, p. 28.

GOOD FRIDAY

As Year A, p. 29.

EASTER EVE

As Year A, p. 30.

EASTER DAY

As Year A, p. 31.

SECOND SUNDAY OF EASTER

As Year A, p. 32.

THIRD SUNDAY OF EASTER

Luke 24:36–48

Let us pray for the peace of Christ in the Church and in the world.

Give grace to the Church to witness through faith to the message of salvation which the Apostles received by sight . . . As he ate with them in his risen body, may the sacrament of his body and blood bring life and healing to all who come.

Grant that the peace of Christ shall bring to an end all disharmony in the world . . . Where there is strife between nations, hostility between races, disputes between individuals, may his presence bring a new and fuller life.

When we gather with our families and friends, keep us open to feel the presence of Christ among us . . . In this community and in all that we do, make us witnesses of the grace that we have received.

Have mercy on all who suffer . . . We pray for those, known to us or unknown, who are sick in body or mind, for the lonely, the homeless, the bereaved . . . May the wounds of Christ's Passion, borne through death to his risen body, be their healing.

We pray for all who have died in the faith of Christ and risen to new life in him . . . May we in our time rejoice with them in seeing him as he is, no ghostly image but the living power of God.

We offer our prayers through Christ in whom the Scriptures are fulfilled.

FOURTH SUNDAY OF EASTER

John 10:11–18

Let us pray for God to be known and obeyed in the Church and in the world.

We pray for the unity of the Church, that all who hold the faith of Christ may be drawn into one fold under one Shepherd . . . Keep the ministers of the Gospel faithful to their calling, to be true guardians of the flock and servants of their Master.

We pray for all who have authority over others, that they may act with justice and mercy, caring for those they govern and protecting them from harm . . . May those who have not known the message of salvation hear your voice and come to rest under your protection.

Give grace to us, to our families, friends and neighbours, to know their Shepherd, to follow him in faith
and find new life in him . . . Grant that this community
shall be well and wisely led and that all her members
may live in harmony.

Have mercy on all who are threatened by the wolves of
war and violence, and on those who suffer from the
wickedness of false leaders . . . Come to all who have
been abandoned by those in whom they trusted, and
lead them back to live again in confidence.

Receive the souls of the departed who have followed
their Shepherd even to the death of the body . . . May
they be one with him in the safety of the heavenly fold
where nothing can do them harm.

We offer our prayers through Christ, the Good
Shepherd who laid down his life for his sheep.

FIFTH SUNDAY OF EASTER

John 15:1–8

Let us pray for constancy and purity in the service of
God.

Grant that the Church may hold fast to her Lord, so that
all her branches may grow together in faith and service
. . . Cleanse her from all that hinders her mission, and
purify her to bring forth the good fruit of the Gospel.

Purge with your compassionate might the corruption
of the world . . . Where there is abuse of power, where
there is selfish exploitation of the weak, where there
is hostility between nations, bring healing and a
new spirit so that all may live in harmony, rooted in
love.

We pray that we may abide in Christ, and his words may abide in us, so that we and all in our community shall be united in him and trust in his strength alone. . . Let us in our work and in our recreation use well the gifts we have been given.

We pray for the outcasts of the world, those who have been cut off from their families, those who have been rejected by society and lost hope of return . . . Restore them to the full dignity of their humanity, and let them grow into new life.

Receive the souls of those who, having borne their fruit in this world, have withered and died . . . May their joy be made perfect in the fellowship of all who have drawn their lives from the eternal vine.

May our prayers be accepted in the name of Christ, the true vine.

SIXTH SUNDAY OF EASTER

John 15:9–17

For obedience to the law of love, let us pray to the Lord.

Give to the Church, chosen and called to service, the love for all which reveals the love of God . . . As she has received grace, may she be a channel of his peace now and for all time.

Grant to those who hold authority the love which is stronger than the love of power . . . May they know that true authority is from above and is fulfilled not in command but in service . . . Grant that love shall drive out hatred between nations and races and the whole world be at peace.

As Christ has called us to be his friends, increase in us

the gift of friendship towards all who come close to us
in our daily lives . . . By our love one for another may
we show that we have heard and answered his call to
follow him.

Have mercy on those who have never known love and
are enslaved by anger and bitterness . . . Show them the
love of God, to restore them to the love of humanity . . .
Hear the prayers of the sick and afflicted who ask for
healing.

We pray for the departed, called to service in this world
and now called to the presence of the Lord who has
loved them from the beginning . . . May their joy be
complete, and may we come to that eternal joy in the
fellowship of the saints.

We pray in the name of Christ who laid down his life
for his friends.

ASCENSION DAY

As Year A, p. 37.

SEVENTH SUNDAY OF EASTER

John 17:6–19

Let us pray for the Church and for the world and thank
God for his love.

Grant that the Church, entrusted with the words of
truth, shall be obedient to her charge and make them
known with zeal and faithfulness . . . Grant that all
Christian people may live their lives fully in the world,
serving its people but not conformed to its ways when
they are contrary to their calling as citizens of heaven.

Bless the world in which and for which Christ died and rose again . . . Give to those in authority the wisdom to know that the world where they have power is not the whole reality, and the grace to use their power for the benefit of those they govern.

Protect from all evil our families, friends and neighbours and let them be sanctified as Christ sanctified himself for those he called his friends . . . May all in our community be guided by the words of truth.

We pray for those whose faith makes them hated and persecuted . . . Bless and strengthen all who have received the words of Christ and sacrificed safety and comfort in their service.

We pray for all who heard the gospel and lived and died in its faith . . . May their joy be complete in the presence of the Lord who has prepared the way for them.

May our prayers be accepted through Christ, whose name is our protection.

PENTECOST

As Year A, p. 39.

TRINITY SUNDAY

As Year A, p. 40.

PROPER 4

Mark 2:23—3:6

For the healing of all ills in the Church and in the world, let us pray to the Lord.

We pray that the Church shall keep holy the Lord's Day in reverence and worship, but never let its observance destroy compassion for those in need . . . Shield your people from hardness of heart and confidence in their own righteousness.

Grant to those in authority the grace not to rule in their own interest but for the good of those they govern . . . May those who make and administer laws have compassion on the weak and lay no oppressive burdens on them.

May we, and all those around us, be alert to perceive where there is need and to give such help as we can . . . Bless our community with the spirit of harmony and mutual concern.

Have mercy on all who are disabled by accident or illness . . . Give them courage and hope in their affliction and bless those who work for their healing.

Receive into new life the souls of those who have departed from this world . . . May they rejoice in the eternal Sabbath where hunger and sickness are no more.

We offer our prayers in the name of Christ, the Lord of the Sabbath.

PROPER 5

Mark 3:20–35

Let us pray to God, the glorious Trinity in unity.

Grant unity to the Church, and strengthen her witness to the gospel faith . . . May all who confess the salvation brought by Christ share his love as sisters and brothers in his name.

Bring unity among the nations, for an end of conflict and distrust . . . Grant that the power which casts out evil shall cause justice to prevail in all places of authority and that the whole world shall know the only source of peace.

Bless us in our families with love for one another that does not fail in times of trouble or disagreement . . . Bless our community with desire for the good of all and the relief of distress.

We pray for all who are troubled with evil passions and are unable to help themselves . . . Grant them release and restoration to a good life . . . Have mercy on families that are divided and bring them back to the love they have lost.

We pray for those who have had fellowship in Christ and have now entered the fellowship of the saints . . . May the love which they knew on earth be made perfect in the love of heaven.

We pray in the name of Christ who casts out all that is evil.

PROPER 6

Mark 4:26–34

Let us pray that the will of God shall be fulfilled in the Church and in the world.

Strengthen the Church to nourish and to spread the good seed of your word entrusted to her care . . . Bless your ministers as they work for the coming of the Kingdom . . . Use them and enable them, so that the harvest may be abundant.

Bring your grace to work silently in the hidden places of the world, to bring to fruition the good that is as yet unknown . . . May your Kingdom come not only through those who have authority but through all the humble and unregarded who seek to live in love and peace.

Come to us in the little things, in the daily round of home and work, in the passing encounters with those we may not see again . . . Bless this community, to be a refuge for the afflicted and a shelter for those in need.

Comfort all who despair because their labour seems to be in vain . . . Give them hope and the strength to persevere until your will for them is completed . . . Bring healing to the sick, peace to the troubled, and comfort to the bereaved.

We pray for all whose lives have grown through this world until the end . . . Grant them new life, fulfilling beyond all earthly understanding the promises in which they trusted and the joy that they have known.

We pray in the name of Christ who brings all things to fruition.

PROPER 7

Mark 4:35–41

For the peace that comes from above, let us pray to the Lord.

Give peace to the Church and take away all that may hinder her ministry . . . Grant to her people the holiness that shall be a refuge and a new hope for all the troubles of the world.

Calm, we pray, the storms that rage in the world . . . Let your word of peace bring an end to the wars and anger that divide nations, and the bitterness that sets people against one another.

Grant that we may hear the voice of Christ and feel his protection in our own lives, and help us to make it known to all whose lives touch ours . . . Where any strife or hurt troubles our community, may it be overcome so that all may live in harmony.

Have compassion on those who have no stability in their lives, who are tossed about by every passing fancy that brings no rest . . . Protect all sailors and all who travel by sea, bringing them in safety to the end of their journeys.

Receive in your mercy the souls of those who have passed from the perils of this world and come to the further shore where all is calm . . . Give them peace and rest, and the new life that begins when their first voyage is over.

May our prayers be accepted through Christ, whose word is healing and calm.

PROPER 8

Mark 5:21–43

Let us pray for healing and fullness of life in the Church and in the world.

Bless the Church with grace to be the channel of peace and renewal for those who suffer, to bring hope in despair and comfort in sorrow . . . Give to all faithful people the wholeness that comes by knowing the presence of Christ.

Look with compassion on to a world long wearied by the sickness of war and the death of the innocent . . . Where the restless multitudes struggle without direction, make known the only source of peace.

Draw us, our families, friends and neighbours, close to the living Christ, to reach out and feel his love . . . Fill our community with the spirit of compassion, to relieve those in need and care for the lonely and those who mourn.

Have mercy on all who are suffering from chronic illness or disability . . . Give them relief in their trouble and guide the skill of those who work for their healing . . . Comfort with your unfailing love the parents who have lost children and all who are bereaved of any they have loved.

We pray for those whose sickness is over and whose sorrow is ended, who are raised from the death of the body . . . Grant us grace in this life to follow in the way of faith and at last to hear the voice that calls to eternal life.

May our prayers be acceptable through Christ, the healer and lifegiver.

PROPER 9

Mark 6:1–13

Let us pray to God for strength and perseverance in his service.

Bless the Church with the spirit of holy poverty, not to trust in wealth or power but only in the enabling of her Lord . . . Make her ministers faithful heirs of the disciples who were first called to perform great works in a strength not their own.

Have mercy on a world where many are so anxious for material things that they do not recognize the better way that is open before them . . . Give to those who hold authority the grace not to be imprisoned in their own power but to see and learn where there is true wisdom.

Give us light to see the gifts of God in all around us, to honour his presence in our families and friends and neighbours . . . Open our hearts and our homes to receive those who are sent to be among us.

Have mercy on all who are sick and bless those who care for them . . . Give them comfort and hope in their affliction . . . Release those who are in the power of evil and restore them to wholeness of life.

We pray for those who have walked in the way of the Lord through this world and have come to their journey's end . . . May they be at peace in the great family of the faithful departed.

We pray in the name of Christ, our Brother and our Redeemer.

PROPER 10

Mark 6:14–29

For the rule of justice and the triumph of mercy, let us pray to the Lord.

Inspire and strengthen the Church to speak out against evil and not to fail in the face of opposition . . . Give to all Christian people the grace to endure when their faith is tested and to bear witness to the truth.

Guide and correct those in authority, that their power shall not be abused and the innocent shall not suffer . . .

Forgive those who support evil policies through fear or ambition, and give them courage to work for good.

Shield us, our families and friends and neighbours, from all anger and violence, whether it comes from among us or from outside . . . Bless those who have influence in this community and give them the will to work for the common good.

Have mercy on all who suffer from injustice, on the weak and vulnerable who are in the hands of oppressors . . . Be close to those who suffer for declaring and practising their faith and save them from their persecutors.

We remember with thanks those who have borne witness to their faith even to death . . . May their witness be our example of constancy until we come to share with them in the life of heaven.

We offer our prayers through Christ, the hope of all who suffer for his sake.

PROPER 11

Mark 6:30–34, 53–56

Let us pray for the peace of God in the Church and in the world.

Grant to the Church the grace to be still and not to lose holiness by being too busy . . . Give her ministers grace to lead their people through the way of quietness into the presence of their Lord.

Speak through the tumult of the world: calm the strident noise of the powerful and the anxiety of the powerless . . . Have compassion on all who wander without direction, and guide them into the paths of peace.

Grant to us, in the pressure of our daily lives, the time to be still, to learn the wisdom that comes in silence . . . Help us to use our leisure well, so that we may have strength to help those whose lives are linked with ours.

We pray for the sick in body or mind, for the injured and the disabled, for those with emotional problems . . . Come to them with your healing power, relieve their afflictions and make them whole.

We pray for those who have passed over the waters of death and come to the shore of eternal life . . . Grant them the peace which this world cannot give and the light which never fails.

May our prayers be heard through Christ, the Shepherd of the lost.

PROPER 12

John 6:1–21

For the feeding of the body and of the soul, let us pray to the Lord.

Bless the Church with grace to teach and nurture all who are committed to her care . . . Accept our offered service, small and weak though it may be, and transform it to be a power for good.

We pray for greater concern for the poor and deprived, for a more compassionate use of this world's goods . . . Grant to those in authority clear vision and caring hearts for the good of all.

Help us, our families and friends, to be confident that

the least we have to give can be greater than we know
. . . Bless with wisdom those who administer the
resources of this community.

Have mercy on all who are hungry, the victims of
famine and the multitude of those who are never
properly fed . . . Strengthen and enable all who work to
bring relief to stricken areas of the world.

We pray for the departed whose need for earthly food
is past . . . Gather them into eternal life, so that nothing
that has been once offered shall be lost.

May our prayers be accepted in Christ, who takes away
all our fear.

PROPER 13

John 6:24–35

Let us pray for God's blessing on the Church and on the
world.

Make the Church a channel for the life that comes from
heaven for the salvation of the world . . . Guide your
people to trust not in the outward signs of success but
in the spiritual power that works silently and unseen.

Be merciful to a world where many are concerned only
for the material needs of life . . . Bless its people with
thankfulness for past mercies and insight to see and follow the new signs of your love for all.

Grant to us, who have been blessed with the gift of
faith, grace to live as those who are fed with the bread
of life . . . Help us to bring our neighbours and those
with whom we work into that holy fellowship.

Have mercy on those who are so burdened by want

and care that they cannot feel the love that could be theirs . . . Come to those who have not known the words of hope, release them from their ignorance and feed them with the bread of life.

We commend to your gracious keeping the souls of those who have died in faith . . . As they received on earth the bread of the sacrament, may they be made perfect as they rejoice in the bread of heaven.

We pray in the name of Christ, the bread of life for us.

PROPER 14

John 6:35, 41–51

Let us pray to God for the eternal life which he has promised to all who trust in him.

Grant that the Church may be always faithful to feed your people with the living bread of the Eucharist . . . Bless her ministers with grace to serve the Kingdom through word and sacrament.

We pray for the world, fed by the life of Christ, for the places where he is not known and the hearts where he is not loved . . . May his sacrifice prevail for the healing of the nations and for peace in all places of strife and violence.

Teach us to recognize the holiness in those around us, in friends and neighbours and all who come into our lives . . . Fill this community with mutual care, for the familiar and for the stranger, as equal children of the Father.

Have mercy on those who are rejected, whose qualities are despised and whose love is not returned . . . Feed with the living bread those who hunger and thirst, in the flesh or in the spirit.

Raise up, in their last day, those who have been drawn back to the loving heart of the Father . . . Give us grace so to follow faithfully in this world that we may rise to the glory of eternal life.

We pray in the name of Christ, the true and living bread.

PROPER 15

John 6:51–58

For the life that comes from above, let us pray to the Lord.

Give grace to the Church faithfully to offer the communion of the body and blood of the Lord, that her people shall be spiritually nourished in receiving it . . . May we abide in fellowship with him and with one another.

As Christ suffered death in the flesh for the life of the world, grant that the people of this present world may find new life in him . . . Bring peace among the nations and in all places where there is strife and violence.

Create in us, in our families, and all around us, the love that grows from the communion of the faithful . . . Make all who live and work in this community worthy of the love by which the living bread was given.

Come in compassion and feed the hungry, whether their hunger be of the body or of the soul . . . Have mercy on all who are afflicted in any way, and bring them healing.

We pray for those who have eaten the bread of life in this world and gone to their rest . . . May they inherit the promise of eternal life given to all who receive it in faith.

Accept our prayers in the name of Christ by whose death we have life.

PROPER 16

John 6:56–69

In the life of the Spirit, let us pray to the Lord.

Keep the Church faithful in word and sacrament to the gospel entrusted to her . . . Make her ministers and her people worthy of the service to which they have been called by the Father.

Bring the light of the Spirit into the world where many trust only in the flesh and walk in darkness . . . Bless those who teach and all those who learn, that the words of truth may be known to all.

Grant that we shall never betray, by word or deed, the faith which we profess . . . Empower us as examples of love to those whose lives touch our own . . . Bless all in this community who are charged with the guidance of others, that they may speak in truth and live according to their teaching.

We pray for those who have lost their faith, who have turned away from the path which they once followed . . . Bring them back, to hear and believe again the words of eternal life.

Receive in mercy the souls of the departed who have walked with their Lord through this world . . . Bring them to eternal life in heaven where he has ascended.

We offer our prayers through Christ, the Holy One of God.

PROPER 17

Mark 7:1–8, 14–15, 21–23

For right judgement in all things, let us pray to the Lord.

We pray that the Church shall be maintained in true holiness, keeping the traditions rightly received and not constrained by human convention and customs . . . Give grace to all Christian people to worship not only with their lips but in their lives.

Guide all rulers and those in authority to govern with both justice and mercy . . . Break through the prejudices which raise barriers between nations and races . . . Bring all people to set aside the things which divide them, and to embrace those which unite them in their shared humanity.

Cleanse us from evil thoughts and desires and from hostility to any whose ways are different from our own . . . Give harmony and a spirit of mutual respect in the life of this community.

Have mercy on all who are enslaved by evil: release them and bring them to a new life of love and service . . . We pray for the victims of prejudice who are persecuted because they do not conform to the expectations of their society.

Receive the souls of the departed into the Kingdom where human strife has ended and worship is made perfect . . . Grant to us all such purity of faith and living that we may in our time be joined with them.

We offer our prayers in desire faithfully to follow Christ as his disciples.

PROPER 18

Mark 7:24–37

Let us pray for wholeness of life in the Church and in the world.

Bless the Church in her universal mission and make her open to receive all who come . . . Give to her ministers the spirit of compassion, and wisdom to discern the needs of those who turn to them.

Have mercy on all in the world who seek for help and are uncertain of their direction . . . Open the ears that have not heard the words of salvation, and loose the tongues that have not learned to praise.

Bless our families with health and strength and with grace to acknowledge the great mercies that we have been given . . . Help us to know and to relieve the troubles of those we meet in our daily lives.

Have compassion on all sick children, and on the parents who grieve for them . . . Come in mercy for the healing of any who are afflicted in hearing or speech . . . Give skill and wisdom to those who work for their relief.

We pray for the departed who worship not through the ears and tongues of flesh but in the fellowship of the spirit . . . May they rest and rejoice in eternal life.

We pray in the name of Christ, who has mercy on all who come to him.

PROPER 19

Mark 8:27–38

In the confidence of faith, let us pray to the Lord.

As the Church proclaims Christ, the Son of God, keep her faithful to his words and his example and make her a witness to his truth . . . Through the way of the Cross, may his people follow in the way of life.

Give wisdom to those in authority, so that they shall not abuse their power but shall honour the good, protect the helpless and spare the innocent . . . May all who pass through this world look beyond their self-interest and find the true source of life.

Grant us patience and courage in times of difficulty and make us ready to share the burdens of those around us . . . Make us ready to deny ourselves for the good of others.

Have mercy on the people whose crosses are heavy with sickness or sorrow, on the dying and the bereaved . . . Bring them comfort and strength in the Lord who trod the way of suffering for the sake of all humanity.

Receive into eternal life those who have ended their lives in this world . . . May the Cross which guided them here be now the sign of their glory.

We pray in the name of Christ, the Son of Man in whom we are saved.

PROPER 20

Mark 9:30–37

In trust and humility, let us pray to the Lord.

Give grace to the Church to be the servant of all . . . Help your faithful people to work together for the Kingdom, seeking no personal honour or reward.

Have mercy on the world where so many are driven on by the desire for power and privilege . . . Break through the pride which exalts nation against nation, race against race, class against class, and restore the innocence that we have lost.

We pray for the children in our families, for all the children in our community and those who teach them and care for them . . . Protect them from harm and lead them into the future that is your will for each of them.

Have mercy on the victims of jealous power and all who are persecuted for the sake of the gospel . . . - Comfort and restore all who are afflicted in mind or body.

We pray for those who have passed through the trials and temptations of this world and are at rest . . . Receive them mercifully into the Kingdom where none ranks before another but all rejoice in one equal glory.

May our prayers be accepted through Christ, who was betrayed and died that we might live.

PROPER 21

Mark 9:38–50

Let us pray to God for his protection and thank him for his goodness.

Keep the Church open to accept and affirm all who work for good . . . Save her from becoming narrow and defensive in her ministry . . . Give to all Christian people willingness to accept as well as to give, and to be gracious in accepting.

Bless and sanctify all human efforts towards a better world . . . Be close to those who have compassion without faith and draw them into your Kingdom.

Give us peace with one another, in our homes and in our work . . . Bless our community with peace and harmony, and cast out all that makes for evil.

Have mercy on children who are damaged and abused; save them and heal the harm they have received . . . Give compassion and courage to those who work for the protection of children.

We pray for the departed, that their sins may be forgiven and that they may be made whole as they enter the Kingdom of Heaven . . . Help us so to live in this world that we may come in purity to eternal life.

We pray in the name of Christ, our hope and our strength.

PROPER 22

Mark 10:2–16

For peace in the Church and peace among all people, let us pray to the Lord.

Give to the Church the innocence of children and the wisdom of experience . . . Guide and bless all who come in childhood, and bring them to the fullness of faith.

Take away the hardness of heart which divides fam-

ilies, breeds strife between people and sets nation
against nation . . . Let the simple trust of a child draw
the peoples of the world together in peace.

As we give thanks for our families, we pray that we
shall never lose our love for one another . . . Bless the
homes throughout this community . . . Guide the
teachers and all who work with children.

Have mercy on those whose lives have been broken by
divorce or separation . . . Heal the wounds they have
suffered, and grant them the spirit of reconciliation and
hope for the future.

We pray for the departed who have entered the
Kingdom where there is no division, but one perfect
union, no strife, but one perfect love . . . Grant to those
who pass through this world the simple faith that leads
to salvation.

We offer our prayers as children of Christ, the protector
of all who come to him.

PROPER 23

Mark 10:17–31

Let us pray for guidance and grace to follow the way to
eternal life.

Make the Church faithful in keeping the commandments and avoiding the temptations of outward success
and power . . . Trusting in no human righteousness but
only in the divine mercy, may your people be as a light
to the world.

Have mercy on the world where so many trust in riches
and seek continually to increase them . . . Guide those

who control the wealth of commerce and the finance of nations, to use their power wisely, setting aside the love of gain and showing compassion for those in need.

Help us, our families, friends and neighbours, to use well the money entrusted to us, whether it is much or little . . . Give grace to those who control the financial affairs of this community that their decisions shall be for the common good.

We pray for all who are enslaved by the passion for material things and have lost their way in the journey of life . . . We pray for the poor of the world, for people and nations in debt, for those whose lives are a daily struggle to survive.

Be merciful to those who have died still trusting in the wealth of this world . . . In the infinite mercy that makes all things possible, receive them and all departed souls into the Kingdom of Heaven.

We pray in the name of Christ, the Teacher of wisdom to all who seek him.

PROPER 24

Mark 10:35–45

Let us pray for right judgement and good desires in the Church and in the world.

Give to the servant Church grace to follow the example of her Lord who came into the world to serve . . . Shield her ministers from pride of place and desire for power, so that when they lead it shall be with humility and love.

Grant that those in authority shall act not as tyrants but with care for the rights of those they govern . . . Draw the nations of the world together in the love of peace and the ending of old rivalries.

Bless us, our families, friends and neighbours, with the spirit of love that seeks no advantage but only the good of all . . . Bless with the same spirit those who make decisions for this community.

Have mercy on all who suffer under tyranny, the nations governed by fear, those who are unjustly treated in their work or in their homes . . . Forgive those who are locked in the struggle for power and bring them to a better understanding.

We give thanks for the departed who have passed from the temptations and dangers of this world . . . May they be forever joyful in the place prepared for them in glory.

We offer our prayers through Christ who gave his life for the ransom of many.

PROPER 25

Mark 10:46b–52

Let us pray that the Church and the world shall be guided to walk in the way of the Lord.

Bless the Church with clear vision to follow wherever the gospel leads . . . Open the ears of all Christian people to hear and respond to those who cry out for the divine mercy.

Give compassion to those in authority, that they may know the needs of those they govern and use their power for good . Enlighten all the people of the world who go on their way unseeing and unguided, and bring them to knowledge of salvation.

We pray for ourselves, that as we pass by on our journey through the world we may not be blind to the needs of those who come close to us . ℞. Bless our community with the spirit of love and concern for one another.

Have mercy on the blind and all whose sight is impaired . . . Bless the doctors who work to save and restore sight, and all who work in places where many suffer from diseases of the eyes.

We give thanks for the departed who have followed the way of faith and come to the end of their journey . . . Grant them, and to us in our time, the perfect vision of holiness in eternity.

May our prayers be accepted through Christ, the merciful Son of David.

or BIBLE SUNDAY

John 5:36–47

In thanksgiving for the holy Scriptures, let us pray to the Lord.

Fill the Church with faith to live as the Bible teaches, and to proclaim the good news of salvation . . . Bless her ministers with the word of power through which all people may be brought to fullness of life.

Bless the work of missionaries and evangelists in all parts of the world . . . Keep them safe from harm and turn the hearts of those who receive them with hostility and suspicion . . . Prosper the work of bible fellowships and societies.

We pray for grace so to read and to hear holy Scripture that our lives, and those of our families and friends, shall be rightly ordered . . . May the word of the Father, revealed through the Son, abide in us.

We pray for all who are persecuted for their fidelity to the word of God . . . Pardon those who through ignorance or ill-will turn the words of the Bible to false purposes, and restore them to the way of truth.

Receive the souls of those who have searched the Scriptures and followed their teaching though the paths of this world, finding in them the glory of God revealed . . . May they enter into the promise of eternal life.

We offer our prayers in the name of Christ, sent by the Father for our salvation.

DEDICATION FESTIVAL

John 10:22–29

Let us renew in prayer our dedication to the service of God.

As we give thanks for this place where we are gathered, we pray that our worship and the worship of the whole Church may be holy and acceptable . . . May your blessing rest upon us and all Christian people, and the whole creation praise your name.

Gather into one fold the people of the world . . . Give strength and perseverance to those who know their Messiah, and open the ears of those who have not heard his voice . . . May all in authority dedicate their power to the common good.

We pray that in our families and in all our lives with others we may share the fellowship that we know in our church . . . Bless all whom we love, and keep them safe in the Father's hand.

In our rejoicing this day we remember all who are afflicted: the sick and injured, the homeless and refugees, the lonely and rejected . . . Have mercy on them, relieve their distress and bring them peace.

We pray for those who have followed their Shepherd to the end of their lives on earth . . . Grant them eternal life in the glory of heaven.

We pray in the name of Christ, who holds us safely in his loving hand.

ALL SAINTS' SUNDAY

John 11:32–44

In fellowship with all the saints, let us pray to the Lord.

We pray that the Church may be worthy of those who have gone before in the faith and left us a pattern of godly life . . . Increase in us the same faith, so that we may see the glory of God and show it forth in our worship.

As we pray for the needs of the world, we ask that those who hold earthly power may know their weakness and mortality, and seek the better way . . . May the prayers of all the saints bring peace and healing to the wrongs of the present time.

Give us the vision to see the holiness in those around us . . . Guided by the example of the saints, may we live our daily lives for the good of all.

Bring comfort to those who mourn; give them hope in

the life that never dies . . . Have mercy on those who are near to death and strengthen them with the courage which upheld the saints in their dying.

We give thanks for all the saints who have died in the faith of Christ . . . May all the departed share with them the blessing of eternal life.

We pray in the name of Christ who gives life to the dead.

FOURTH SUNDAY BEFORE ADVENT

Mark 12:28–34

Let us pray for the love of God to be known in the Church and in the world.

Give grace to the Church in keeping the commandments of love, to honour the Lord and to serve his people . . . May our offering of worship be made holy by obedience.

Bring peace in the disputes and uncertainties that divide people and nations . . . Grant to all in authority reverence for God and care for those they govern.

Strengthen us in true love for our neighbours, for all who are close to us in our homes and in our work . . . Bless all in this community to live together in the spirit of love and mutual respect.

Have mercy on those who have never known love or have lost the love which they once had . . . Make whole again the lives that have been damaged by quarrels and resentment.

We pray for those who in this world have sought to live in obedience to the commandments . . . Receive them

into the Kingdom where the supreme and only rule is
the rule of love.

We pray in the name of Christ who has given us the
great commandments.

THIRD SUNDAY BEFORE ADVENT

Mark 1:14–20

Let us pray for the coming of God's Kingdom in the
Church and in the world.

Keep the Church ever obedient to the call of God, to
fulfil the mission entrusted to her . . . Bless with
strength and perseverance those who are called to be
ministers of the gospel.

Bless those who have gone out into the world, forsak-
ing much for the sake of the gospel . . . May their
message be heard for the peace of the nations and for
peace in human hearts.

As we go to our daily work, keep us mindful of the faith
to which we have been called . . . Make us ready to
serve others and to tell the good news of the Kingdom.

Have compassion on those who are lonely when loved
ones have gone away to follow new paths of life . . .
Give them assurance of the divine love that is always
with them, and the human love which endures in
absence.

We pray for those who have ended their work in the
world and come to the Kingdom . . . Let the voice which
first called them to faith now call them home to glory.

May our prayers be accepted through Christ who calls
us to follow him.

SECOND SUNDAY BEFORE ADVENT

Mark 13:1–8

Let us pray for God's peace in the Church and in the world.

Keep the Church vigilant against error and false doctrine . . . As we give thanks for our places of worship, help us to remember that all earthly things will pass away . . . Teach us to be faithful in the Temple of the Spirit.

Have mercy on the world where nation rises against nation and the hearts of many are torn with anger . . . Bring the blessings of peace where there is war and violence . . . Protect your people from those who by abuse of power would deceive and lead astray those they govern.

Grant clear sight to us, to our families, friends and neighbours, that we may discern the truth and not fall into false ways . . . Give integrity and sureness of purpose to those who hold authority in this community.

Visit and relieve all who are suffering from natural disasters, the victims of famine and the victims of human aggression . . . Lead back into the right way all who have been brought to sorrow by following false leaders.

We pray for those who have come to the end of life in this world . . . Grant them peace in the world where there is no strife or danger, but joy that will not pass away.

We offer our prayer through Christ, in whose name alone we put our trust.

CHRIST THE KING

John 18:33b–37

For the peace and the power of the Kingdom, let us pray to the Lord.

Inspire and strengthen the Church to work for the coming of the Kingdom . . . Keep her ministers faithful in teaching the word of their Master and King.

Look with compassion on the world where people seek to resolve their differences by anger and aggression . . . Guide the leaders of the nations to follow the way of peace.

In our times of work and our times of rest, help us always to live as servants of Christ the King . . . May his loving power prevail in our families and among all who live in this community.

Have mercy on all who have been betrayed and abandoned by those they trusted . . . Comfort and save those who are falsely accused, and stand alone before the powerful who have no pity.

We pray for the departed who are no longer subject to the kingdoms of this world . . . Grant them light and peace in the Kingdom of Heaven where Christ reigns in eternal glory.

We pray in the name of Christ, who was born to be our King.

Principal Service

Year C

FIRST SUNDAY OF ADVENT

Luke 21:25–36

Let us pray for grace as we prepare for the coming of the Lord.

Keep the Church faithful to heed your warnings and to trust in your promises . . . Make her ministers ever watchful to protect your people against evil and to lead them into the way of truth.

Look with compassion on the world where many are weighed down by care and trapped in the desire for ever-increasing pleasure . . . Heal the hostilities which divide nations, and bring to the whole earth the blessing of peace.

Lift up our eyes to see the signs of our redemption at this present time . . . When troubles distress us, give strength to us, to our families, friends and neighbours, and free our hearts from fear.

We pray for all who are afflicted, for the victims of war and violence, for those in peril from natural disasters . . . Bring the calm of your presence to all whose lives are stunted by fear and anxiety.

Receive into eternal life the souls of all who have passed through the dangers of this world and come to their rest . . . Keep us mindful that after the death of the body we shall stand before the Son of Man, and grant us mercy in that day.

We pray in the name of Christ, whose words will not pass away.

SECOND SUNDAY OF ADVENT

Luke 3:1–6

Let us pray that God will grant us true repentance and forgiveness of sins.

Empower your Church to speak with the prophetic voice that proclaims the way of salvation . . . Fill all her people, in their different callings, with zeal to be ministers of the gospel.

Grant to the rulers of this world the spirit of humility and the gift of discernment, that their power may be exercised for the good of all . . . Make straight the crooked ways in which so many walk astray, and make smooth the rough places of bitter strife.

Help us to use this Advent time well, to hear again the call to repentance and the message of salvation . . . Lead all who live and work in this community into the paths of peace.

We pray for the sick and injured, for the lonely and neglected, for those who mourn, known to us or unknown . . . Bring them comfort in their afflictions and guide the efforts of those who work for their relief.

We pray for those who in the flesh saw the salvation of God and have entered into its perfection . . . Give us grace to follow them in the way prepared for those who seek the Kingdom.

May our prayers be accepted through Christ who has united us with himself in baptism.

THIRD SUNDAY OF ADVENT

Luke 3:7–18

Let us pray that the way of the Lord may be followed in the Church and in the world.

We pray that the Church shall never rest complacently on past blessings but shall for ever desire to know and to fulfil her present calling . . . Give her ministers wisdom to instruct all who come for guidance.

Bring harmony in the disputes and jealousies that keep people apart . . . Bless with the spirit of justice those who have power over others, and help them to do their duty according to what is right.

Guide us in our daily work and in all our relationships, so that the faith we profess shall be seen in our lives . . . Make us thankful for what we possess and generous to share with those in need.

Have mercy on all who are oppressed and unjustly treated . . . Relieve all who are crushed by heavy taxation and kept poor by the greed of those who rule them.

Receive the souls of the departed who in this life sought to bear good fruit in the name of their Master . . . Gather them into the harvest of heaven where all doubts are ended and all truth made plain.

We offer our prayers in the name of Christ who baptizes with the Spirit and with fire.

FOURTH SUNDAY OF ADVENT

Luke 1:39–55

Joyful in the presence of the Lord, let us pray for the Church and for the world.

Prepare the Church to receive with joy and thanksgiving the coming of the Lord at his Nativity . . . May all
Christian people join with Mary his Mother to proclaim
his greatness.

Raise up the lowly ones of the world and give them
fullness of life . . . Be merciful to those who are deceived
by power and wealth . . . Do not send the rich empty
away.

As we prepare again to celebrate this Christmas time,
bless us, our families, friends and neighbours, with
purity of spirit and holiness of desire . . . Shield us from
selfish pleasure, make us mindful of the needs of many
in our community.

We pray for all who are hungry, whether for food to
sustain their bodies or faith to nourish their souls . . .
Comfort and heal those who through sickness or
poverty can feel little joy at this time.

We pray for the departed who have magnified their
Lord on earth and now praise him in his heavenly
Kingdom . . . May they find their eternal joy in the
company of the Blessed Virgin Mary and all the saints.

We pray in the name of Christ, Son of God and son of
Mary.

CHRISTMAS DAY

As Year A, p. 5.

FIRST SUNDAY OF CHRISTMAS

Luke 2:41–52

In the love of the Holy Family, let us pray to the Lord.

Keep the Church in holy obedience, to follow the

example of Christ in his boyhood . . . As we worship together in our Father's house, may our offering be made with wisdom and reverence.

Grant to those who are powerful in the world the grace to learn from the simple and innocent . . . Bless all children; give them secure homes and a happy growth towards maturity.

In our family lives, set ever before us the life of the Holy Family as our pattern of love . . . Bless the homes in this community with peace and joy at this season.

Look with compassion on parents who have lost children, by death or estrangement or any cause . . . Grant that the grace which filled the home at Nazareth may be for the healing of homes that are damaged and divided.

We pray for those who have passed away from their homes on earth and found their eternal home in heaven . . . Grant them peace with Mary and Joseph and all the saints.

May our prayers be accepted through Christ, the eternal Son of the Father.

SECOND SUNDAY OF CHRISTMAS

As for Year A, p. 7.

THE EPIPHANY

As for Year A, p. 8.

THE BAPTISM OF CHRIST

Luke 3:15–17, 21–22

Through the water of baptism and in the power of the Spirit, let us pray to the Lord.

Keep the Church faithful in following the teaching and example of her Lord . . . Give her ministers grace to instruct and to baptize all who come to be made members of the Body of Christ.

May the Holy Spirit break through the uncertainties and questionings of the world and lead all people into the way of truth . . . Grant repentance and new endeavour to any who are in error through false teaching.

We give thanks for our baptism, and pray for grace to fulfil the vows we have made at the baptism of others . . . Bless all who are preparing for baptism, especially those who live in our community, and their parents and godparents.

Have mercy on all who have lost the faith which they had and have turned away from their allegiance . . . Restore to them the assurance and hope which they once knew.

We pray for the departed who came to new life through the water of baptism and have passed over the river of death . . . Mercifully receive them into the life that will not end.

We offer our prayers through Christ the Beloved Son of the Father.

SECOND SUNDAY OF EPIPHANY

John 2:1–11

Let us pray for the Church and for the world, and let us thank God for his bounty.

Give grace to the Church to make known and to share the wonderful gifts which God has given her . . . Help her ministers to serve all who come to seek her blessing on their marriages. *L. ın ẏ. M.*   *HAITI E'QVAKE*
                                                                        /VICTIMS,
We pray for the needs of the world, that those who *KESE,*
have plenty shall be gracious in giving, and that those *RELIEF*
who have too little shall be supplied . . . Wherever people rejoice together, may the power of divine love be felt among them. *L ın Ẏ m*

We pray for all who are newly married or preparing for marriage, remembering especially any known to us . . . *AḍN ᴨᴠ*
Bless our own families and those around us with the gracious presence of Christ. *L ın Ẏm*   *ILL ANIỌ ın*
                                                                       NEEỌ OF YOUR STRENGTh
Look with compassion on all who are ~~distressed~~ *+ SUPPOₑ₂*
~~because they cannot meet the needs of those they love~~
. . . Come with healing to those whose marriages are broken or in danger and restore the trust with which they began their lives together. *L ıᴴ Ẏ m*

Have mercy on all who have received the gifts of ~~God~~ *(K)*
in this world and have passed to their rest . . . Grant them a place at the eternal marriage feast of heaven, in the company of Christ, his Mother and all his saints.
                                               LıN Ẏ m
We pray in the name of Christ who has revealed his glory to the world.

MERCIFUL FATHER,

THIRD SUNDAY OF EPIPHANY

Luke 4:14–21

In the power of the Spirit, let us pray to the Lord.

Enrich the Church by the gift of the Spirit, to prophesy and interpret the abiding words of the holy Scriptures . . . Bless her ministers and all who preach the faith; grant them wisdom and power in their work.

Give grace to all who are in positions of authority to lead public opinion . . . Grant that those who hear shall discern between the true and the false, for the peace of the nations and goodwill among all people.

Help us to hear and to follow the word of God and to share it with all whose lives touch our own . . . Bless and direct the teachers and all who give instruction in our community.

Grant release to those who are held captive by human tyranny or by the tyranny of sin . . . Restore sight to the blind and freedom to the oppressed, and make the good news known to the poor.

We give thanks for the souls who have received the freedom and the perfect sight of the faithful departed . . . Help us so to follow in the way of revelation that we at the last may enter into eternal life.

We offer our prayers through Christ, in whom the Scriptures are fulfilled.

FOURTH SUNDAY OF EPIPHANY

Luke 4:21–30

In the light of his glorious revelation, let us pray to the Lord.

Grant that the Church shall offer her worship in holiness and reverence . . . Give her the spirit of prophecy, to make known the message of salvation and to praise the mighty works of the Lord.

Come in power and love to the people who walk in darkness, and lighten the dark places of the world . . . Give the grace of understanding, that all may delight in the innocence of the young and listen to the wisdom of the old.

Bless our families, when we come to worship and when we are together in our homes . . . Guide those who care for the old people in our community.

Have mercy on widows and widowers and all who mourn the loss of those they have loved . . . Comfort the mothers who suffer anguish for the troubles of their children . . . Lighten the darkness that closes around the dying.

We pray for those who have died and now rejoice in a greater light than this world can give . . . Grant that we in our time may depart in peace and find salvation.

We pray in the name of Christ, by whom our inner thoughts are known.

THE PRESENTATION OF CHRIST

As Year A, p. 13.

EPIPHANY 5 (PROPER 1)

Luke 5:1–11

Let us pray for the Church and for the world, and let us thank God for the abundance of his mercy.

Bless the Church with power to preach the word at all times and in many places . . . Give to her ministers the courage and the guidance to launch out into the deep and draw many into the fellowship of believers.

Grant the grace and wisdom by which the resources of the land and of the sea may be used for the good of all . . . We pray for those who go out into the deep waters, that they may be preserved from danger and that their labour may be blessed.

Keep us, our families and friends, confident and comforted in the presence of the Lord . . . Bless all who work in this community, and give them a sense of purpose in their calling.

Come in compassion to those who have lost hope, to all discouraged by continual failures, to those who see no return for their work . . . Give pardon and assurance to any who fear that their sins have cut them off from salvation.)   *SICK & ALL IN NEED*

We pray for those who have finished their work in this world and have come to the farther shore . . . Bring them through the deep water of death and draw them into the great harvest of the redeemed.

May our prayers be accepted though Christ, who never departs from repentant sinners.

EPIPHANY 6 (PROPER 2)

Luke 6:17–26

Let us pray to God for his blessing on the Church and on the world.

Guard the Church in holiness and keep her safe from the snares of worldly power and success . . . May she herself receive, and also bring to many, the blessings promised in the gospel.

Come in mercy to those in authority, to the rich and to those who hold themselves in high esteem . . . Save them from the errors of pride; give them the humility which works in love and service for others . . . Grant to the poor of the world relief to enable them to live with full human dignity.

Keep us mindful of the many blessings we have received and give the same grace to our families, friends and neighbours and those with whom we work . . . Grant clear vision and right judgement to all in this community.

We pray for the sick, the sorrowful, the hungry and those in need . . . We pray for those who are slandered and persecuted for their faith . . . Have mercy on their affliction and grant them the healing touch of your love.

We pray for those who after the joys and the sorrows of this life have found their reward in heaven . . . Grant that our lives here may be pure and holy and that at last we may be joined with them.

We offer our prayers in the name of Christ, the divine Healer of all ills.

EPPHANY 7 (PROPER 3)

Luke 6:27–38

In love and fellowship with all, let us pray to the Lord.

Fill the Church with the spirit of mutual love which seeks no advantage but only the glory of God . . . Help her ministers to speak the truth in love, patiently to bear opposition and to admonish without condemnation.

We pray for peace in the world, for reconciliation between nations and races that are hostile to one another . . . Turn curses to blessings and anger to loving acceptance. Guide those who have much of this world's goods to share more freely with those who have little.

Give grace to us, to our families, friends and neighbours, to live in love and peace, to resolve all disputes. and to forgive all injuries . . . Bless with a generous spirit all who live and work in this community.

Have mercy on all who are oppressed, who suffer violence and contempt . . . Strengthen them in their trouble and turn the hearts of their persecutors.

We pray for those who have passed out of this world, and are at rest from its wraths and sorrows . . . Grant them forgiveness of sins and the reward of eternal life.

We pray in the name of Christ, ever loving and merciful to all who call on him.

SECOND SUNDAY BEFORE LENT

Luke 8:22–25

Let us pray to God for the peace which he alone can give.

Grant that the Church shall follow in the way of her Lord, to bring peace and love to all who come . . . Increase her faith and let her not fear the power of any evil.

Calm the angry passions which shake the world . . . Bring peace where there is war, calm where there is hostility and tension . . . Guide those who have rule over others into the way of peace.

We pray that when the storms of anger begin to rise among us we shall hear the voice of the Lord and live in harmony . . . Bless our families and all around us with confidence and peace of mind.

Give hope and courage to those who live in fear and do not walk in the way of peace . . . Shield from danger all who travel and bring them safely to the end of their journeys.

We pray for the departed who have been brought through the storms of this world to the haven of eternal life . . . May they rest in peace and see the glory of their Lord.

We offer our prayers in the name of Christ who has all things at his command.

SUNDAY BEFORE LENT

Luke 9:28–43

Let us pray that the glory of the Lord may shine on the Church and on the world.

On the heights of worship and in the duties of daily life, keep the Church ever faithful . . . Grant that we, his disciples at this present time, may share the awesome joy which the first disciples felt in the company of their Lord.

Give to all in authority and power the desire to stand aside from the demands of their position and reflect quietly about the responsibility which they bear . . . May the wisdom and holiness of the past prevail for the guidance of the world today.

Day by day, in our homes and in our work, grant us the vision of glory in simple things around us . . . Teach us to know that in every situation it is good to be there because the Lord is with us.

Touch with your healing power the sick and afflicted and give strength to those who minister to them . . . Give times of refreshment and peace to those whose lives seem too full for them to find space for the things of the spirit.

We pray for the departed, that in the company of patriarchs and prophets and all the saints, they may enter into eternal life . . . May the light of heaven shine for ever upon them.

We offer our prayers in the name of Christ the King of Glory.

ASH WEDNESDAY

As Year A, p. 20.

FIRST SUNDAY OF LENT

Luke 4:1–13

Let us pray for the saving power of God in the Church and in the world.

Keep the Church vigilant against all temptations and make her perfect in the service and worship of God . . . Filled with the Holy Spirit, may all Christian people keep this Lenten time with penitence and amendment of life.

Cleanse the world from the temptations of greed, of power and of pride . . . Guide those in positions of authority to know their weakness and be compassionate to the needs of others.

Bless us at this time with grace to make and to keep a good rule of life, during this Lent and beyond . . . Be ever close to us, to our families, friends and neighbours, to shield us from temptation and lead us in the right way.

Have mercy on all who are greatly tempted to harm themselves or others . . . Free them from the power of evil and bring them out of the wilderness into the good land of faith.

We give thanks for the departed who have passed through the temptations of this world and come safely to their rest . . . May they rejoice in the company of the saints and of all the angelic host.

May our prayers be accepted through Christ, our guardian against temptation.

SECOND SUNDAY OF LENT

Luke 13:31–35

For protection from all perils and temptations, let us pray to the Lord.

Gather the Church under the wings of divine love and keep her in holiness . . . Bless her witness, and make her a sure refuge for all who seek salvation.

We pray for the world, for the great cities and the lonely villages, for every place where people find shelter and comfort . . . Preserve them in peace, guard them from danger, cast out all evil.

Bless our homes and make them places of joy for our families and welcome for guests . . . Bless all in this community who care for the deprived and the homeless.

Have mercy on victims of violence and all who suffer for their faith . . . Visit and heal the sick in mind and all who are in the grip of evil power.

Receive into eternal life the souls who have ended their life on earth and have come home to be with their Lord . . . Lead us on through the dangers of this world until we may rest under the wings of mercy.

We pray in the name of Christ whose love calls us to his side.

THIRD SUNDAY OF LENT

Luke 13:1–9

Let us pray to God for mercy upon the Church and the world.

Grant to the Church the spirit of sincere repentance for all offences . . . Make her fruitful in the service of the gospel for the salvation of God's people.

We pray that all who hold power in the world shall exercise it with mercy and compassion for those they govern . . . Bless the labours of all who work to produce and to meet other human needs.

Bless us in our daily work, that it may be done to the glory of God . . . Bless those with whom we work, and all who work in our community.

We pray for those who toil and see no result for all they do . . . Have mercy on all who have suffered from accidents and disasters and sustain those who minister to them.

Receive into new life those who have come to the end of their earthly work and are gathered into the company of the departed . . . Be merciful to those who have died unprepared and without repentance for their sins.

May our prayers be accepted through Christ who tenderly nurtures his children.

FOURTH SUNDAY OF LENT

Luke 15:1–3, 11b–32

Let us pray to God, our loving Father in heaven.

Keep the Church ever open to receive in love all who come with faith to seek the divine mercy . . . As we worship here, shield us from pride and complacency in fulfilling our duty and make us remember that we too are sinners.

We pray for the world where the love of money tempts many to turn aside from the right way to waste themselves in empty and useless living . . . Bless with a forgiving spirit all who have power to restore or to reject those who have erred and offended.

Grant to us, in our families and in our friendships, grace to remember the mercy we have been given and to remain in harmony and love with any who have offended us . . . Bless all the homes in our community with perfect harmony and love.

Look with compassion on families where there is estrangement . . . Grant that quarrels shall be mended and love renewed . . . Have mercy on all who have left their homes and now seek in want and loneliness the way to return.

We pray for the departed who have walked through the temptations of this world and have come home . . . May they rejoice in the fellowship of the redeemed who died and are alive again.

We pray in the name of Christ, the refuge of sinners who come to him in penitence and faith.

or MOTHERING SUNDAY

As Year A, p. 25.

FIFTH SUNDAY OF LENT

John 12:1–8

Let us pray in reverent faith for the Church and for the world.

Grant that the Church, anointed with the oil of gladness in the faith of her Lord, may ever honour his majesty and proclaim his saving love . . . May his people so meditate upon his Passion that they may live worthily of the redemption which he brought.

Bless the people of this world with the spirit of generosity, not to count the cost of compassion but to give freely in love . . . We pray that those who perform the works of mercy shall be upheld and strengthened.

Give grace to us, our families, friends and neighbours, to enter this Passiontide with love for one another and repentance for our sins . . . Bless all who live or work in this community with the spirit of service and mutual care.

Have mercy on the poor and neglected, the homeless, those entrapped by debt . . . Lead back into the right way those who have fallen into dishonesty and betrayed the trust that was placed in them.

We pray for the departed who have lived with Christ and followed him in death . . . May they be anointed with the precious ointment of eternal life . . . May we so live in this world that our lives shall be a preparation for a holy death.

May our prayers be acceptable through Christ, the Messiah, the Anointed One.

PALM SUNDAY

As Year A, p. 27.

MAUNDY THURSDAY

As Year A, p. 28.

GOOD FRIDAY

As Year A, p. 29.

EASTER EVE

As Year A, p. 30.

EASTER DAY

As Year A, p. 31.

SECOND SUNDAY OF EASTER

As Year A, p. 32.

THIRD SUNDAY OF EASTER

John 21:1–19

In the power of the Resurrection, let us pray to the Lord.

Grant that your Church may ever respond with joyful eagerness to the vision of her risen Lord . . . Empower her ministers faithfully to feed your sheep, and bless all

Christian people with grace to follow Christ to the end of the way.

We pray for the world where so many are as sheep that are not fed, some lacking food for the body and others food for the soul . . . Grant that all people may come to know the Lord who is calling them to his side.

As we give thanks for the mercy that fulfils our daily needs, we pray that we shall remember the needs of others and be generous in giving help . . . Help us to love our Lord with all our hearts and to live our family lives in fellowship with him.

We pray for all who are disappointed after much striving that has seemed to end in failure . . . Give them new hope and purpose in their lives . . . Be merciful to those who have lost the love they once knew, and bring them back into the way from which they have strayed.

Receive the souls of the departed who have followed Christ and been with him at the end . . . Gather them into the fold of the redeemed, into the company of the heavenly feast.

We pray in the name of Christ who calls us to himself as his children.

FOURTH SUNDAY OF EASTER

John 10:22–30

Let us pray for the Church and the world, held in the almighty hand of God.

As our Lord walked in the Temple on the Feast of the Dedication, so may his Church be renewed in dedication to his service . . . Strengthen her ministers to be good shepherds in their care of his flock.

We pray for those in authority, and for all people . . . Gather them into one fold, that all nations and all races may live together in peace.

Be close to us, our families and friends, and hold us safely in the hand of the divine protection . . . Give harmony and mutual care to all who live or work in this community.

Have mercy on those who wander in the world, unsure of their way and not knowing in whom to put their trust . . . Come with healing love to all who are sick and afflicted in body or mind.

We pray for the departed who have heard and responded to the voice of Christ in this world . . . Grant them the eternal life that is promised to all who follow him in penitence and faith.

We pray in the name of Christ who calls his sheep to be at his side.

FIFTH SUNDAY OF EASTER

John 13:31–35

Seeking the glory of God in all things, let us pray for the Church and for the world.

Fill the Church with grace, that God may be glorified in her worship . . . Keep all Christian people faithful to the great commandment of love.

Give to the people of the world a new spirit, of love in place of anger, of trust in place of suspicion . . . Grant that those who lead the nations may know the responsibility they bear, and work for peace.

We pray that we, with our families, friends and neighbours, may be held together in the bond of love

... Help us to offer ourselves, as witnesses to the glory of God.

Pardon and restore those who have failed in love and betrayed their trust . . . Have mercy on all who suffer from the unfaithfulness of any who are dear to them . . . Comfort and support the innocent who are betrayed into the hands of unjust powers.

We pray for the departed who in this life put their trust in Christ . . . Lead them now to go where their Master has gone, to live with him in glory.

May our prayers be accepted through Christ, the Son of Man for ever glorified.

SIXTH SUNDAY OF EASTER

John 14:23–29

For the peace which comes from above, let us pray to the Lord.

Keep the Church in peace, and draw all believers together into one unbroken love . . . Guided by the Holy Spirit, may her ministers proclaim the gospel by word and example.

Grant peace to the world, peace among nations and races, peace in the hearts of all people . . . Bless those who hold authority, and incline their wills to seek peace and to maintain it.

We pray that the Lord may be with us and make his home in our homes . . . Keep us in love and respect for all those who are near to us in family, work or friendship . . . Give to all in this community the blessing of peace and harmony.

Have mercy on all who suffer where peace is broken,
on the victims of war and violence . . . Have mercy on
those who experience domestic violence, and grant that
love shall prevail and drive away anger.

We pray for those who have passed through death
from the troubles of this world . . . Receive them into the
peace of eternal life, where their Lord has gone before.

May our prayers be heard through Christ who gives us
his peace.

ASCENSION DAY

As Year A, p. 37.

SEVENTH SUNDAY OF EASTER

John 17:20–26

In unity of faith, let us pray for the Church and for the
world.

Come in mercy to the Church, that her members may
be made one, for the purity of her worship and the
strengthening of her witness to the gospel . . . May all
Christian people be ministers of the divine glory.

We pray for the peace of the world, for the harmony of
races and nations . . . We pray that all people shall come
to know the Lord and find their peace in him.

As we have received the gift of faith, help us to share it
with those who are near to us . . . May the powerful love
of God be the support of our families and friends and of
all in this community.

Have mercy on people and communities torn apart by religious conflict . . . Heal their divisions and unite them in mutual love.

We pray for those who have come to the end of their journey in this world . . . Grant them to be with the Lord they have loved and to see his glory.

May our prayers be accepted through Christ, who calls us to be one in him.

PENTECOST

As Year A, p. 39.

TRINITY SUNDAY

As Year A, p. 40.

PROPER 4

Luke 7:1b–10

Let us pray with confidence, trusting in the power of God.

Fill the Church with faith, that the words of healing may be spoken through her . . . Keep her ministers and leaders mindful of their responsibility to serve in humility for the sake of the gospel.

We pray that all who hold authority in the world shall know that they serve a higher power than their own, and exercise their rule with mercy . . . We pray for all in military service who seek to keep their faith in the midst of conflict.

Although we are unworthy that you should come under our roof, bless our homes with your presence . . . Give to us, to our families, friends and neighbours, the spirit of compassion for one another in times of need.

Bring healing to the sick in mind or body . . . Give skill to those who care for them, and comfort to those who sorrow for their pain . . . Have mercy on all who are close to death, and ease their passing.

We pray for all who have left the pain and sickness of this world and are at rest . . . May they be made whole in the glory to God.

We offer our prayers in the name of Christ, by whose word our souls are healed.

PROPER 5

Luke 7:11–17

Let us pray to God for the needs of the Church and the world.

Guide and strengthen the Church to live the new life of the gospel . . . Give grace to her ministers to serve in love and humility, and faithfully to preach the word of God.

Hear our prayers for the people of the world in the trials and sorrows of their daily lives . . . Heal the divisions which tear nations and races asunder . . . Grant that wisdom and compassion shall guide all who are in authority.

We pray for our families, friends and neighbours . . . Protect them from harm, guide them in temptation and comfort them in trouble . . . We pray for the wellbeing of all who live and work in this community.

Have mercy on all who mourn, the widows, the orphans, parents who have lost children . . . Bless them with the healing touch of love and the hope of resurrection.

Receive into rest and peace the souls of those who have died to this world and risen to new life . . . Keep us firm in faith, that we may be brought at last into the fellowship of the redeemed.

We pray in the name of Christ, the power of resurrection to eternal life.

PROPER 6

Luke 7:36—8:3

Let us pray to God, who knows the unspoken secrets of all hearts.

As our Lord accepts the offering of sinners and outcasts given in love, so may the Church, the company of sinners who know their need, seek where their only help is to be found . . . May his people honour him by offering the most precious gifts of reverence and holy obedience, and receiving in love all who turn to him.

As God has shown mercy to the whole world in pardoning the debt of sin through the atoning death of his Son, may the spirit of love prevail to pardon the debts under which so many are burdened . . . We pray for the countries that are working to build a new life on the broken foundations of the past, and for compassion in the rich who can help to make them free.

When we sit at meals with our families and our friends, help us to remember that the Lord is always present . . . May our lives, and the lives of all in this community, be such as will honour that presence with the best that each can offer.

We pray for all who are bowed down and broken through debt that has gone beyond their means . . . We pray too for all who are burdened with sin and are ignorant or afraid to come for pardon . . . May the power of Christ, who knows the inmost self, enter and heal them.

Receive into eternal life the departed who with tears of repentance have come to the feet of Christ, and those who in this world have failed to know the fullness of his love for sinners . . . May the infinity of that love embrace them all.

As the precious ointment was offered in humility, love and sorrow, we bring our prayers to the feet of Christ.

PROPER 7

Luke 8:26–39

Let us pray for the healing of all ills in the Church and in the world.

Cleanse the Church from all that may hinder her witness to the gospel . . . Give grace to her ministers and to all Christian people, that they may make known the mighty works of God.

Have mercy on the world where many are in conflict with one another and are not at peace within them-selves . . . Come with the healing Spirit which drives out evil in the high places of power and in the lives of simple people.

Bless us, our families and friends, with inward calm and love for one another . . . Help us to care for those among us who are distressed in any way . . . Give serenity of mind to all who live and work in our community.

Look with compassion on all who are disturbed in their minds . . . Give skill and patience to those who care for them and seek to heal them . . . Comfort those who are rejected by society, and restore them to the fellowship that has been denied them.

We pray for the departed, and especially those whose lives in this world have been troubled by mental illness . . . May they be made perfect in the heavenly peace which passes understanding.

We pray in the name of Christ, who casts out all that is evil.

PROPER 8

Luke 9:51–62

Let us pray in confidence for the coming of God's Kingdom.

Shield the Church from all pride and love of power, that the gospel may be proclaimed with humility and love for all . . . Grant perseverance in service to her ministers and to all who have put their hands to the plough of faith.

We pray for any in authority who are tempted to misuse their power over others . . . May there be justice with mercy through all the world, and peace among the nations.

Bless us with constancy in our duties to one another, to our families, friends and neighbours and those with whom we work . . . May our lives together be a following in faith of the way where we are led.

We pray for the homeless, for refugees and all who have no place to lay their heads . . . Have mercy on those who have recently been bereaved, and give them comfort in their loss.

Receive in mercy the souls who have passed on their way and departed from this world . . . As their bodies have been laid to rest, grant that their souls shall rise to eternal life.

May our prayers be accepted through Christ as we seek to follow in his steps.

PROPER 9

Luke 10:1–11, 16–20

Let us pray to God in confidence for the coming of the Kingdom.

Bless the Church with the spirit of true discipleship . . . Give grace to all Christian people to show in their lives the healing power of the gospel . . . Bring new labourers to hear the call and work for the harvest of the Lord.

We pray that all nations may know the peace that comes from above . . . Drive out the evil which brings strife between people, give light to the dark places and fill the world with knowledge of the truth.

Let our homes be as those which have been visited by the messengers of peace and love . . . Make us welcoming and hospitable, open to learn from any who come into our lives.

Grant healing to the sick in mind and body, and skill to those who care for them . . . Defend and strengthen all who have gone forth as missionaries to face opposition and danger.

We pray for the departed who have laboured for good in this world . . . May their names be written in heaven and their joy be everlasting.

We pray in the name of Christ, by whose power evil is overcome.

PROPER 10

Luke 10:25–37

Let us pray that the law of love shall prevail in the Church and in the world.

May the Church be obedient to the great commandments of love for God and for all people . . . Keep her ministers faithful in their calling, and shield them and all Christian people from failing in care for those who need their help.

We give thanks for the grace which moves people to help one another and overcome differences of race and nation . . . Take away the prejudices which cause division, and fill all human hearts with compassion.

Keep us watchful and ready to give help when it is needed, whether in our families, to our friends or to strangers . . . In our community we pray for the emergency services and all who give help to those in distress.

Have mercy on the victims of crime, on all who suffer violence from strangers or from those near to them . . . Bring healing to the injured and restoration to the outcast.

We pray for the departed who have come to the end of their journey . . . May they be healed from all the wounds of this world and made whole in the peace of heaven.

May our prayers be accepted through Christ, the source of love and compassion.

PROPER 11

Luke 10:38–42

Let us draw near to God, and pray for the Church and the world.

Keep the Church steadfast in faith, failing neither in worship of her Lord nor in service to his people . . . Bring all Christian people to sit at his feet and hear his word.

We pray for the people of the world who are occupied in many things and deaf to the voice of calm . . . Bless those who serve others in their material needs and those who serve them through prayer.

Make our homes places of welcome where those who enter may find rest and refreshment . . . In our daily work, grant us space to be still and know the presence of the Lord.

Look with compassion on all who are stressed and wearied by the pressure of their lives . . . Bring healing and renewal to those who have been broken by over-work.

Receive in mercy the departed who have finished their work in this world . . . Grant rest to the weary and joy to the troubled, as they come into the eternal presence of their Lord.

May our prayers be accepted through Christ in whom we find the better part.

PROPER 12

Luke 11:1–13

Let us pray with confidence to our Father in heaven.

Hear the prayer of the Church for her work and worship, as we look to the coming of the Kingdom ... Keep all Christian people faithful in prayer, trusting that as we ask so we shall receive.

We pray that the will of God shall be done through all the world, until its people are made one in him ... We pray for a new spirit among nations, that disputes shall be ended, differences reconciled and debts forgiven.

Come in blessing to us, to our families, friends and neighbours, and give us what we need day by day ... Give grace to all in our community, to share generously the good things we are given with those who have little.

Pardon and heal all who are caught in bitterness and resentment about wrongs that they cannot forgive ... Deliver from evil those who are sorely tried as they make decisions for their lives.

Receive in mercy the souls of the departed and forgive the sins of their lives on earth ... Grant them peace and joy for ever in the Kingdom of Heaven.

May our prayers be accepted in the name of Christ, who has taught us how to pray.

PROPER 13

Luke 12:13–21

Let us pray for the Church and for the world, that in all things they may be rich towards God.

Shield the Church from temptation to seek the wealth and power that pass away . . . Bless her with the true wealth which makes her a faithful servant, eager to fulfil his word.

We pray for the rich of the world, that they shall be spared from the dangers of pride and moved to use their wealth for the general good . . . Grant wisdom and justice to those who must make decisions in conflicting interests.

When we are at ease with our families and friends, let us never forget that all we enjoy is a gift from above . . . Help us to be thankful for what we possess, free from greed for what we do not have, and generous in what we are able to give.

Bring relief to the poor who have suffered from the greed of the rich, as individuals or as whole nations . . . Have mercy on those who have been overcome by foolish greed and brought to ruin.

We pray for all who have died suddenly and un-prepared . . . May the abundant mercy of divine love receive them into life . . . Teach us to live as souls that are ready for the call of God.

We pray in the name of Christ, our only hope and assurance.

PROPER 14

Luke 12:32–40

Let us pray that God will guide us, and bring us through obedience to his Kingdom.

Keep the Church always ready to respond to the call of God and to serve with zeal and humility . . . Grant that her ministers shall be faithful stewards of the spiritual treasures entrusted to them.

Give healing to the world where many are oppressed by concern for material things . . . Guide those who command and those who serve, that each shall live in harmony and seek the good of all.

Be with us in our daily work and bless those who work with us . . . May all who serve our community be watchful to give help where there is most need.

We pray for all whose work is hard, who toil for little reward and grow weary . . . Sustain them in their tasks, bring them hope, and give compassion to those who have power over them to ease their burdens.

Have mercy on those who have been called from this world . . . Grant them peace and a share in the unfailing treasure of heaven.

We offer our prayers through Christ, the Master who became the servant of all.

PROPER 15

Luke 12:49–56

For peace and unity in the Church and in the world, let us pray to the Lord.

Grant unity to the Church, healing the divisions which hinder her work and witness . . . Guide her people to discern the signs of the present time and give them strength to persevere in the service of the gospel.

Bring the leaders of nations to a common purpose and a desire for peace . . . Give them wisdom to avoid conflict while there is yet time, that all people may live in security without fear of war.

We pray that love and harmony shall prevail in our homes and in the homes of our friends and neighbours . . . Make us channels of peace when we meet anger and disputes in our work and with any whose lives touch our own.

Look with compassion on broken families . . . Grant reconciliation in the quarrels that have severed those who were once united in love . . . Bring back to their homes those who have left them in anger.

We pray for all who have departed this life . . . Have mercy on those who died unreconciled, and give them the peace which they could not find on earth.

May our prayers be accepted in Christ, who gives us his signs to guide us.

PROPER 16

Luke 13:10–17

Let us pray for the Church and for the world and thank God for his healing love.

Grant that the Church, in keeping due reverence and order, shall never be turned aside from works of aid and compassion . . . Accept her worship, and strengthen her in prayer for all who need healing in mind or body.

We pray for the world where conflict arises from small matters grown into great disputes . . . Give wisdom to all in authority, that they may judge with mercy, discerning the needs of those they govern.

Bless us, our families and friends, in our daily work . . . Be near us in times of difficulty and make us ready to help others who are in any kind of trouble.

Have mercy on the sick who have suffered for many years without relief . . . Give hope to the disabled, help them to fullness of life and empower those who care for them.

We pray for the departed who have been freed from the trials and limitations of the body . . . Receive them into the new life where there is no suffering, and where the redeemed are made perfect in the divine love.

We offer our prayers in the name of Christ, who sets us free from all evil.

PROPER 17

Luke 14:1, 7–14

In love and concern for all people, let us pray to the Lord.

Keep the Church constant in the humility of the service to which she is called . . . Bless her ministers as they work to spread the good news of salvation to all.

Be merciful to the world where many are possessed by pride and made arrogant by power . . . Grant that those who have authority may exercise it with equal regard for the dignity of all whom they govern.

Bless our homes and make them places of welcome . . .
Keep us from becoming narrow in our hospitality, and
help us to look beyond those who are nearest to us.

We pray for all who are slighted and ignored because
of their poverty, their disability or their personal problems . . . Fill our community with love for the needy and
concern for the common good.

We pray for the departed who have come to the
Kingdom where all are made equal through grace . . .
Help us so to live in this world that we may be worthy
at last to receive with them the blessing of eternal life.

May our prayers be accepted through Christ, the Lord
of the humble and meek.

PROPER 18

Luke 14:25–33

For perseverance in faith and service, let us pray to the
Lord.

Bless the Church with resolve to hold nothing back
from the duty to which she has been called . . . Fill her
ministers with zeal for the gospel and strengthen them
to follow where their Master has led.

We pray for the world where many strive for mastery
and put their trust in the outward signs of power and
wealth . . . Lead the rulers of nations into the way of
peace, to seek settlement before confrontation.

Bless our families, friends and neighbours with wisdom and discernment in all their decisions . . . As we
give thanks for the human love that we have been
given, we pray that it shall never cause us to neglect our
love and duty to God.

Have mercy on all who have been ruined by their own folly and wrong judgement . . . Relieve their need and restore them to the good life which they have lost . . . Forgive those who have been false to the faith they once professed, and bring them back into the right way.

We pray for the departed who have sought to follow the way of Christ through this world and have endured to the end . . . Receive them into the peace where all perils are past and all burdens are laid down.

We pray in the name of Christ who calls us to follow him as his disciples.

PROPER 19

Luke 15:1–10

Let us pray that God will guide the Church and the world into the right way.

Strengthen the Church in compassion and love, to seek the lost and restore the fallen . . . Make her ministers loving shepherds of the flock and guardians of the gospel treasure.

Give grace to all who hold power in the world, that they shall not despise or neglect any who come under their authority . . . We pray for all who are in the wilderness, for those who are scattered abroad where nations have been broken and identities lost.

Fill us with love for our neighbours and all who come near to us in our daily lives . . . Help us to share their sorrows and join in their rejoicing . . . Grant wisdom and patience to those who care for the needy in our community.

Have mercy on those who have lost their way, whose

lives are broken by sin or suffering . . . Bring them safely home, to find again all that they have lost and rejoice with those who have loved them.

We pray for the departed, for those who have strayed in this world and those who have followed in faith . . . Gather them into the one fold of your love and grant them eternal life.

May our prayers be accepted through Christ, who calls us to repent and return to him.

PROPER 20

Luke 16:1–13

Let us pray to God that his majesty shall be honoured in the Church and in the world.

We pray that the Church shall serve diligently in all things, proclaiming the gospel without fear or flattery of any . . . Grant that her ministers and all Christian people shall be for ever single-minded in their allegiance to the faith.

Give to all in authority the grace to temper justice with mercy and use their power with equal regard for all . . . Be with those who are engaged in business and finance, that they may work with integrity and render a just account in all things for which they are responsible.

Bless us with honesty in our daily lives and with concern for the needs of those with whom we work . . . In all our relationships, keep us faithful to the law of love. *for I another.*

Be merciful to those who are without work, whether by fault or misfortune . . . Give hope to those who have long been idle and have fallen into despair . . . Guide and relieve all who are burdened with debt.

We pray for those who have ended their labours and been called to their last account . . . Receive them into the life of heaven where no temptation can stain the purity of worship and delight.

We offer our prayers in the name of Christ, our only Master.

PROPER 21

Luke 16:19–31

For love, healing and salvation, let us pray to the Lord.

Defend the Church from the temptation to seek influence with the rich and powerful . . . Inspire her ministers to preach the gospel of God's equal love for all, to stir the indifferent and give hope to the humble.

We pray that those who are rich in this world may be generous in giving from their abundance for the relief of those in need . . . Open the way between the prosperous and the poor nations, for material aid and better understanding, that the whole world may live in peace.

As we give thanks for the comforts of our life, keep us mindful of the needs of others . . . Give us grace to see and respond when we can give help to those near to us, or those whose lives briefly touch our own.

Look with compassion on the poor, the hungry and the homeless . . . Bring healing to the sick, especially those whose affliction makes them despised by others . . . Bless those who work for the relief of poverty here and in all the world.

We pray for the departed, especially for those who did

not learn the lesson of unselfish love in this world . . . In the infinite mercy of God, may they too find peace with all who have suffered and come to rest . . . Help us so to live that we shall be received into eternal life.

May our prayers be accepted through Christ, the source of all compassion.

PROPER 22

Luke 17:5–10

Let us pray that all may be obedient in the service of God.

Increase the faith of the Church, that the saving power of your love may be proclaimed . . . Give to all Christian people the grace to be obedient servants, seeking no reward but the joy of following your will.

Guide those in authority to serve those they govern and to set their needs above their own desires . . . May all work be dedicated to the common good and the peace of the world.

Bless us in our daily work, and bless those who work with us . . . Knowing that we are not worthy in ourselves to make any offering, let us seek so to live in faith that our service shall be made acceptable.

Have mercy on all whose work is heavy, those who labour day after day with little reward . . . Give rest to the weary, food to the hungry and strength to those who have lost hope.

Receive into life those who have laboured in this world until the end . . . Grant them a place at the heavenly feast, and bring us in our time to share the joy that is prepared for those who die in faith.

We offer our prayers in the name of Christ, our Lord and Master.

PROPER 23

Luke 17:11–19

Let us pray, with thanksgiving to God for all the blessings of this life.

Empower the Church to be a refuge for all people, a beacon to all the nations . . . Keep her ministers always ready to receive and comfort those who come to them for any kind of help.

Bring reconciliation wherever there is conflict between faiths and races . . . Grant the spirit of peace, that none may be despised for their status or condition but all may be drawn into a single harmony of life.

We pray for our families, friends and neighbours, for shared sympathy and mutual help . . . Make us duly thankful for all the benefits we have received . . . Bless and strengthen all who work for the abandoned and homeless in our community.

Grant healing to the sick and skill to those who work for them . . . We pray particularly for those suffering from chronic illness and for those who are shunned because of their affliction.

We pray for those who have come through tribulation and suffering in this world, to be made whole in heaven . . . Give to them and to all the departed the eternal life of the faithful.

May our prayers be accepted in the name of Christ, the merciful Healer.

PROPER 24

Luke 18:1–8

Let us pray to God for right judgement in all things, and thank him for his goodness.

Keep the Church constant and faithful in prayer . . . Give to all Christian people grace to spread the good news of the hope they have received.

We pray for all who exercise judgement in the world . . . Make them patient in hearing and impartial in deciding . . . Lead to peaceful agreement all who are at enmity over legal disputes.

Make us just in all our dealings, honest in our work, compassionate towards those who need us . . . Bless all in this community who are engaged in legal work.

Have mercy on all who suffer injustice, the victims of false judgements or the indifference of those from whom they seek redress . . . Bring comfort and support to widows and orphans in their need.

We pray for those who have passed from this world and come to judgement . . . Be merciful to them, hear our prayers and grant them eternal life.

We pray in the name of Christ, the righteous Judge of all.

PROPER 25

Luke 18:9–14

May God direct our prayers and lead us in the way of humility.

Shield the Church from pride and complacency . . . Give to all your people the wisdom to know that they are not worthy to raise their eyes to you, but are saved by mercy and not by merit.

We pray that the powerful and privileged in the world shall know their frailty and not put their trust in themselves . . . Bless those who work with money and those who deal with taxation: keep them honest and compassionate in all they do.

Grant to us, to our families, friends and neighbours, true humility, recognition of our own faults and the grace to value others more highly than ourselves . . . Guide those who plan and control the finances of our community.

Visit and relieve all who suffer from heavy burdens of taxation, or are in want through the false dealing of others . . . Bring release to all who are caught in the snare of their own dishonesty and cannot find a way of escape.

We pray for those who have departed from this life . . . Look with mercy on those who were proud in this world and those who were humble . . . Forgive their sins and receive them into the joy of heaven.

Accept the prayers which we offer through Christ, who pardons our unworthiness.

or BIBLE SUNDAY

Luke 4:16–24

Let us pray for the Church and for the world, and let us thank God for his holy word.

Fill the Church with zeal and wisdom in proclaiming

the message of the Bible . . . Give grace to those who preach the word of salvation: may they speak in the power of the Spirit.

We pray that the world may be brought to knowledge of the truth . . . Take away hostility and suspicion, so that all may be valued for themselves and not for their race or nationality.

Help us to share with those around us the good news that we have received . . . Bless all in this community who seek by teaching and example to lead people into the right way.

Have mercy on the sick and afflicted, the poor and the homeless . . . Give them such relief in their bodily needs that they may be open to the healing of the spirit.

We pray for those who have worshipped here, have heard the words of life and come to their rest . . . May they enter into the eternal worship of heaven, according to the promise of the Scriptures.

We ask that our prayers shall be heard through Christ, in whose words we trust.

DEDICATION FESTIVAL

John 2:13–22

For renewal of faith and reverence, let us pray to the Lord.

Give to the Church a firm resolve to maintain her places of worship in the beauty of holiness . . . Fill this building with light and joy for all who come . . . Drive out all that is not holy.

We pray for fair and honest dealing in the business of

the world . . . Grant that none shall seek to benefit by the
loss of others but that all shall be done with desire for
the common good.

Grant us zeal to renew our faith, to dedicate ourselves
and our families again to the service of God . . . Bless all
in this community who are engaged in trade: keep
them in the way of truth.

Look with compassion on all who suffer from the greed
and injustice of those who have power over them . . .
Turn the hearts of those who follow evil ways and
bring them back to honest living.

We pray for all who have worshipped in this place and
gone to their rest . . . Make perfect the service which
they offered here, and grant them eternal life.

We offer these our prayers, dedicated in the name of
Christ.

ALL SAINTS' SUNDAY

Luke 6:20–31

In the fellowship of all the saints, let us pray to the
Lord.

Give the Church strength to challenge the false values
of the world and to show the way to salvation . . . Bless
her ministers in their work . . . Empower them to spread
the gospel by teaching and by example.

Have mercy on those who are rich in this world and do
not know their inner poverty; on those who are
filled with material pleasure and do not know their
emptiness . . . Bless all in authority with wisdom and
discernment to lead their people in the right way.

Give grace to us, our families, friends and neighbours, to know where true joy is to be found, to grasp it and to share it . . . In all things may we do to others as we would have them do to us.

We pray for all who are afflicted, for the poor and hungry, for those who are oppressed and persecuted . . . Bring them relief in their need, and bless the work of those who seek to help them.

Receive in mercy the souls of the departed who have passed from the joys and sorrows of this world, and grant them eternal life . . . Help us so to live that we may share with them, and with the saints, the life where all hurts are healed and all wrongs are righted.

May our prayers be accepted through Christ, the Lord of all saints and the source of every blessing.

FOURTH SUNDAY BEFORE ADVENT

Luke 19:1–10

Let us draw near to God, to pray in confidence and faith.

Fill the Church with zeal to come ever closer to the presence of her Lord . . . Grant her ministers grace to make known the good news of salvation to those who are far off and to those who are near.

We pray for a world that desires security and comfort but does not know where true joy is to be found . . . Give compassion to those who hold power in the rich nations, that they may bring relief to the nations that are burdened with debt.

Let us know the presence of Christ among us, to make

us generous in our hospitality, welcoming in our homes . . . We pray for those who are responsible for the financial affairs of this community.

Have mercy on those who have been led into evil ways through greed for riches . . . Open their hearts to work with love and integrity in their dealings . . . Come to the aid of those who have fallen into debt and see no way of release.

Receive in mercy the departed who have sought to know Christ in this world and have come to his nearer presence . . . May they join in the heavenly feast with the faithful of all times and places.

We pray in the name of Christ who came to seek and save the lost.

THIRD SUNDAY BEFORE ADVENT

Luke 2:27–38

In the faith of resurrection to eternal life, let us pray to the Lord.

Endow the Church with grace to interpret the Scriptures rightly and to proclaim the resurrection faith . . . Help her ministers and all Christian people to guide into the right way those who are uncertain and seek assurance.

Bless those in authority, that they may govern wisely and for the common good . . . Bring into the way of truth all who are too confident in their knowledge and are leading themselves and others into error.

Grant to our families, friends and neighbours to be contented in our homes and sensitive to the needs of those we meet . . . Guide with sound judgement those who teach and give advice in our community.

Visit and comfort all who are bereaved . . . Have mercy on those who are caught in difficult relationships and on the families that are broken . . . Bring them new hope and understanding.

We pray for those who have died and become children of the resurrection . . . Grant them a place with the patriarchs and prophets, the saints and angels, and all the faithful departed.

May our prayers be accepted through Christ, the Lord of eternal life.

SECOND SUNDAY BEFORE ADVENT

Luke 21:5–19

For fidelity and perseverance, let us pray to the Lord.

Keep the Church faithful in trouble as well as in prosperity . . . Guide her ministers to discern the signs of the time and to strengthen their flock . . . By the light of the Holy Spirit, may all Christian people be empowered to testify to the truth.

We pray for the world that is torn by conflict in many places . . . Give wisdom to all in authority, that they may know the perils that lie in power, and may govern for the good of all.

Make us true and constant in all our relationships . . . Bless us, our families, friends and neighbours with mutual love and care for one another, to share our problems and find comfort in one another.

Have mercy on the victims of war and violence, and

those who suffer from natural disasters . . . Strengthen those who are persecuted for their faith, give them hope in their trouble and turn the hearts of those who oppress them.

We pray for those who have endured to the end and are freed from the dangers of this world . . . Grant them rest and peace, in the Kingdom where the Lord is the Temple that will never be destroyed.

May our prayers be accepted through Christ, the source of all wisdom.

CHRIST THE KING

Luke 23:33–43

In penitence and faith, let us pray for the Church and for the world.

Grant that the Church shall be worthy of the sufferings of her Lord, shall honour him in worship and serve him humbly in his people . . . Give her ministers grace to declare the forgiveness of sins to all who are penitent and to comfort those who are in despair.

Bless all who are in authority, that they shall rule with mercy and with respect for those who are under them . . . We pray for soldiers, and for all who must carry out the works of judgement.

Be with us, with our families, friends and neighbours at this time . . . As we come near to celebrate the birth of our Lord, help us to remember his suffering for our sake and to sorrow for our sins even as we rejoice in his glory.

We pray for all who suffer from the cruelty of power

. . . Lead back into joy those who seek pardon for their sins . . . Give peace and comfort to those who are near to death.

Receive the souls of those who have died in faith, and look with compassion on those who have died without repentance . . . May the everlasting mercy open the gates of Paradise when we have passed from this world.

We pray in the name of Christ, the King who reigns from the Cross.

Other Days in the Church's Year

NEW YEAR: NAMING AND CIRCUMCISION OF JESUS

Luke 2:15–21

At the birth of the year, let us pray for the Church and for the world.

May the Church for ever praise and honour the holy Name of Jesus her Lord . . . As the shepherds told of his Nativity, let all Christian people glorify God and bear witness to his love.

We pray for the needs of the world, remembering especially those whose work is hard, that they may be given strength and joy . . . Grant to those in authority the light of wisdom and the grace to govern with care and justice.

Bless us, our families, friends and neighbours, with the love which was in the Holy Family . . . We pray for the children in this community, that they may be safe from all harm and grow in happiness.

Have compassion on all who suffer in body, mind or spirit and cannot feel the joy of this season . . . Bless all who are in despair and have lost their way, that this new year may be for them a new beginning.

Receive in mercy the departed who came like Jesus to human birth and have ended their lives in this world . . . Grant them a place in the eternal worship of heaven where all is praise and glory.

We pray in the name of Jesus Christ, the Name above all names.

ROGATION DAYS

Matthew 6:1–15

Let us pray to God with sincerity and truth.

Grant to the Church that holiness which shall make her prayers acceptable . . . May her good works be done in quiet and humility, so that the glory may be for God alone.

Bless the earth with abundance of food and bless human wills with care for its just distribution . . . As all desire the daily bread which sustains the body, so may all learn to seek the grace which nourishes the spirit.

Be close to us, our families, friends and neighbours, in our times of prayer . . . Help us to be generous to those in need and grateful for all that provides for our lives.

Have mercy on all who live in anxiety about their bodily needs . . . Bring new hope to the places where life is hard and labour poorly rewarded . . . Grant to those who harbour resentment for wrongs done to them the grace to forgive, so that they may be forgiven.

We pray for the departed who have served and worshipped in this world and have gone to their rest . . . May our prayers for them be heard, and joined with the everlasting worship of heaven.

We pray in the name of Christ, who has taught us how to pray.

THANKSGIVING FOR HOLY COMMUNION

John 6:51–58

Let us pray to God, with thanksgiving for our communion with him.

As the Church has been granted the privilege of this wonderful sacrament, may she be always faithful to the command of her Lord to do this in remembrance of him . . . Keep her ministers and people reverent in celebrating and receiving the holy communion.

May the people of the world be brought to know and to honour the life that is offered in the bread and the wine . . . Give wisdom to all in authority, that they may rule as those who know that the true power comes from above.

Keep us, our families, friends and neighbours, faithful to the truth we have been taught and grateful for the grace we have received . . . May we and all who are near to us be sustained by the living bread.

Have mercy on those whose bodily hunger keeps them from caring for the things of the spirit . . . Come to them in their need, relieve their suffering and make their lives whole.

We pray for the departed who have been fed with the bread of life in this world and have gone to rest . . . Raise them up and grant them the promised eternal life.

We pray in the name of Christ, the true and living Bread.

THE BLESSED VIRGIN MARY

Luke 1:46–55

Let us pray that the grace of God shall fill the Church and the world.

Guide your Church to follow the example of the Blessed Virgin Mary in patience, humility and trust . . . As we honour her for the sake of her beloved Son, grant that all Christian people may know and make known the gentle love that he knew in his human family.

Grant that men and women may honour one another in the wholeness of our restored humanity . . . Bless the women who are working for peace and justice in the world . . . Use their service of kindness and compassion to reconcile the places of strife and anger.

As we pray for our families, friends and neighbours, we pray especially for the mothers among us . . . We ask for blessing on the ministry of women in this church and in all the churches . . . We pray for all who work with maternal care in our community.

Have mercy on women suffering from cruelty and violence . . . We pray for women in societies where they are despised and treated as unequal . . . We pray for those who are unhappy and ill-treated in their families.

We join our prayers with the prayers of the Blessed Virgin Mary for the departed . . . In the hour of death, may we too be raised to eternal life and enter into their fellowship.

We pray in the name of Christ, son of Mary, Son of God.

HARVEST Year A

Luke 12:16–30

Let us pray for the Church and for the world, and let us thank God for his bountiful gifts.

May the Church, trusting in the will of God, be shielded from anxiety and doubt . . . May she be faithful to fulfil his purpose for a rich harvest of the spirit.

We give thanks for the love which brings food from the earth for the life of all its creatures . . . We pray that those who control the natural resources of the world shall be wise in their management and generous in their allocation.

Give us grateful hearts for the good things which we have received and for the joy of sharing them with others . . . Bless and guide those who provide for the daily needs of this community.

Look with compassion on the poor and hungry; grant them relief in their need . . . Have mercy on the rich who have become complacent for themselves and indifferent to others . . . Bring them to understand where the true values are to be found.

We pray for the souls who have been called to their account and left behind the anxieties of this world . . . Grant them rest and peace in the company of all the faithful.

We pray through Christ, who cares for our daily needs.

HARVEST Year B

Matthew 6:25–33

For the needs of the Church and of the world, let us pray to the Lord.

Guide and strengthen the Church to seek the Kingdom and to show the way of salvation . . . May all Christian people give thanks for the good things of this life, but look beyond to the greater glory.

We pray for the world where many are anxious only for their material needs . . . Give light to those who walk in the darkness of their fears for the unknown future . . . Bless with a rich harvest those who work in farming and fishing.

Forgive our anxieties and lack of trust . . . Help us to bring hope by word and example to those around us . . . Grant sufficient for their need to all who live and work in this community.

Look with compassion on the places where the harvest is poor and famine threatens . . . Give strength to all who work to relieve those who are hungry.

We pray for those who have departed from this world . . . Receive them into the eternal Kingdom where fear is ended and where none shall hunger and thirst again.

We pray in the name of Christ, casting all our cares upon him as he cares for us.

HARVEST Year C

John 6:25–35

Let us pray for God's blessing on the life of the Church and of the world.

Grant that the Church may so hunger and thirst after righteousness that she may bear faithful witness to the love of God . . . Give grace to her ministers worthily to offer the bread and the wine of salvation.

As the people of Israel were wonderfully fed in the wilderness, may the needs of all the world be satisfied . . . Give wisdom to those in power, to make just distribution of food and drink for the common good.

Give grace to us, our families, friends and neighbours, to seek the Lord with grateful hearts and to serve him in pure love . . . Bless this community with concern for all its members in their bodily and spiritual needs.

We pray for those who have too little for their sustenance, for all who suffer because they cannot feed their families . . . Bless those who seek to make the deserts blossom and the barren places fertile.

Grant rest and peace to those who have left this world and hunger no more . . . May they and all the faithful departed be fed with bread of heaven.

We offer our prayers through Christ, who gives us the food of eternal life.

COMMEMORATION OF THE FAITHFUL DEPARTED

John 5:19–25

For the living and dead, let us pray to the Lord.

May the Church on earth be united in faith with the Church Triumphant in heaven . . . Give grace to all Christian people to follow the good examples of the faithful in past ages . . .

Help the people of the world to remember that they are mortal and that the works of their hands will not endure for ever . . . May that knowledge draw them together in closer fellowship while their time on earth remains . . . Guide all in authority to respect the wisdom of the past.

As we pray for our families and friends, we give thanks for those we have loved and see no more, and for the generations from which our lives are drawn . . . Help us so to value all those who are near to us, that when we depart from this life they shall remember us with love.

Have compassion on the bereaved . . . Grant them the support of human love, and faith in the Resurrection to sustain them as they continue their lives . . . We pray for those who are near to death at this time, that they may be comforted and their passing be easy.

Receive the souls of the departed who have passed their brief time in this world and returned to the Giver of life . . . Look not upon their sins but upon the loving face of the Son who died and conquered death . . . Grant us at last the grace to die trusting in that love.

We pray in the name of Christ, whose death has given us life.

SAINTS' DAYS

John 15:1–8

Let us pray to God, whose saints have shown his glory in the Church and in the world.

Guide your Church to follow the example of blessed *N* and of all your saints through the ages, and to witness with joyful praise and reverent worship . . . May her ministers and all her people know that they too are called to holiness.

Sanctify all human striving towards a better world, that all may work together for good . . . Give wisdom to all in authority, to learn from those who in the past have governed with justice and mercy.

In all our families, with our friends and at our work, help us to share the grace which we see in the life of Saint *N* . . . Bless our community with the love that seeks peace and perfection for all.

Have compassion on those who suffer for the truth . . . May they find strength in the example of Saint *N* . . . Open the vision of holiness for the comfort of all who are afflicted in mind or body.

We give thanks for blessed *N* and for all who have left us a pattern of holy living . . . Give us grace to honour their memory not only with our lips, but in lives that make us worthy to come with them to eternal life in the heavenly glory.

May our prayers be accepted in the name of Christ who calls his people to be saints.

Special Occasions

(The Revised Common Lectionary does not include readings for these additional services. The yearly lectionary to accompany Common Worship *has a choice of readings: one of the Gospels suggested for each occasion has been selected here.)*

THE GUIDANCE OF THE HOLY SPIRIT

John 14:23–26

For the guidance of the Holy Spirit, let us pray to the Lord.

Send the Holy Spirit upon the Church, that she may truly believe and faithfully teach the words of salvation . . . Bless her ministers with discernment, and strengthen them in their proclamation of the gospel.

Give wisdom to the rulers of the world and all in authority, that they may use their power in the right way . . . May the Holy Spirit fill the world, to bring peace and unity among the nations.

Make our homes holy places, fit to be the homes of the divine presence . . . Bless and guide all who make decisions in this community.

We pray for those who have not known the love of God or have lost the love they once had . . . May the Holy Spirit lead them back into truth . . . Bring comfort to all who are afflicted in body or mind.

We pray for those who have departed from this life . . . In mercy, guide their souls on their way, and bring them home to the eternal love of heaven.

We make our prayers in the name of Christ through whom the Holy Spirit has come and dwells among us.

MISSION AND EVANGELISM

Matthew 5:13–16

Let us pray to God for the growth of his Kingdom.

Give to the Church grace to shine as a light in the world and show forth the glory of her Lord . . . Bless her ministers with power to preach the gospel of salvation . . . Grant strength and perseverance to all Christian missionaries, evangelists and teachers.

Hasten the time when the earth shall be filled with the knowledge of the Lord . . . Bring the light of truth to all in positions of authority and influence, that they may lead those they govern into the right way.

Help us so to live that our deeds shall be worthy of the faith which we hold . . . In our community, bless all teachers and those who can be a guide to others.

We pray for all who suffer for their witness to the faith, for missionaries in hostile countries, for converts who are persecuted by their communities . . . Have mercy on those who have fallen away, and restore in them the confidence of their first love.

Receive into eternal life the departed who in this world have tried to live by faith and to share it with others . . . May the light that was in them be drawn into the light of heavenly glory.

We pray in the name of Christ, our light and example.

THE UNITY OF THE CHURCH

John 17:11b–23

Let us pray to God for the unity of the Church and for peace in the world.

Through the faith shared by all Christian people, bring the whole Church into unity . . . Forgive our outward divisions, and draw us together as a greater witness to the gospel which we proclaim.

Grant to all people a new unity of purpose for the preservation of the earth and the service of the common good . . . Give peace among the nations, between races, and in each human heart.

We pray for our friends and neighbours, and all who share our faith but not our worship . . . Help us to learn from them, to see our imperfections and to work with them for the good of our whole community.

Look with compassion on all places in the world that are torn by religious strife, and relieve the victims of violence . . . May contempt give way to respect, and hostility to understanding.

We pray for the departed who have worshipped in many ways and ended their earthly service . . . Bring them to the joy of heaven where all are one in the divine glory.

We unite our prayers with the prayer of Christ that we may all be one.

THE PEACE OF THE WORLD

Also suitable for Remembrance Sunday

John 14:23–29

For the peace of the Church and of the world, let us pray to the Lord.

Fill the Church with mutual love among her members, for her greater witness to all people . . . May the Holy Spirit guide them into the paths of peace.

Give peace among the nations and between races . . . Where there is hostility bring understanding, where there is suspicion bring trust . . . Grant to all in authority the will to work for peace and a better world.

Bless us, our families, friends and neighbours, with the spirit of peace . . . Help us to live in harmony and concern for one another . . . Bless all in this community with the peace that comes from above.

Have mercy on the victims of war and violence, the wounded and the bereaved, the refugees and dispossessed . . . Give power to those who work to repair the hurt of war.

We pray for all who have died in war, whose deaths were sudden and unprepared . . . Grant them the peace which was denied them on earth, and raise them to new life.

We offer our prayers through Christ, who gives us his peace.

SOCIAL JUSTICE AND RESPONSIBILITY

Matthew 5:1–12

Let us pray to God for the welfare of all his people.

Strengthen the Church to confirm her preaching of the gospel by compassion and example . . . Bless your people with grace to act with mercy, to be peacemakers and to live as servants of all.

We pray that human rights shall be respected and that all people shall live in love and harmony . . . Give to rulers and all in authority the spirit of justice and responsibility towards those they govern.

In all our lives make us sensitive to the needs of those around us . . . Bless all who work for welfare in this community.

Have compassion on all who are deprived and oppressed, all who lack the basic needs of life for themselves and their families . . . Visit and relieve those who are persecuted for their beliefs.

We pray for the departed, especially those whose lives have been hard and weary . . . Receive them into the joy of heaven where all are equal in their blessedness.

May our prayers be accepted in the name of Christ, who bestows his blessings on all who come to him.

MINISTRY, INCLUDING THE EMBER DAYS

Luke 12:35–43

Let us pray to God for the ministry of word and sacrament.

Bless the Church with faithful servants for the proclamation of the gospel and the work of the Kingdom . . . Grant that those who hear the call to ministry, as clergy or laity, may follow it in love and truth.

Bless those who have authority in the world . . . Teach them to rule with justice and seek the common good . . . Give light to all people, to find and honour their vocation in life, that the divine purpose may be fulfilled.

Help us to offer ourselves for whatever ministry is required of us . . . In our homes and in our work, in all that we do, may we live as faithful servants of our Lord and of other people.

Have mercy on those who have lost their sense of vocation, and those who have been disappointed and turned away from the ministry they desired . . . Lead them into the way that is right for them, and strengthen them with new purpose.

We pray for the servants of God who have completed their tasks and gone to their rest . . . May they rejoice in the heavenly feast and may we so follow our calling here that we may at last be joined with them.

May our prayers be accepted through Christ who has called us to his service.

IN TIMES OF TROUBLE

Luke 12:1–7

Let us pray to God for his mercy on the Church and on the world.

Keep the Church steadfast and faithful to her calling among all the trials and difficulties of this time . . . Bless her ministers with grace to give strength and comfort to those in trouble.

We pray for a troubled world, distressed by wars and fear of war, where nations rise against nations and races against races . . . Bring peace and reconciliation, give calm to the angry and courage to the fearful . . . Unite all people in compassion for each other.

Bless us, our families, friends and neighbours, with the assurance that we are loved and all our needs are known . . . When we are distressed and anxious, teach us again that at the last all shall be well.

Have mercy on all who are afflicted, the sick in mind or body, the victims of natural disasters or of human evil . . . May the love that cares for the least of creatures be their hope and their relief.

We pray for those who have been taken from the troubles of this world and are at rest . . . May their joy be complete in the glory of heaven.

We pray in the name of Christ, our hope and refuge in all our trouble.

FOR THE SOVEREIGN

Matthew 22:16–22

Let us pray to God that the Church and the world shall be governed according to his will.

Grant that the Church may be well and wisely governed . . . Guide those who hold authority to remember that they are called as servants . . . Keep all Christian people as faithful subjects of their countries, while always seeking the greater Kingdom.

We pray for all rulers and leaders, for their guidance in the ways of wisdom, justice and peace . . . Bless Elizabeth our Queen and all the Royal Family . . . Protect them from all evil and strengthen them in their duty.

We pray that we shall reach out in love to all whose lives come near to our own . . . Where we have influence, help us to use it well, where we must obey, help us to obey willingly . . . Bless and guide all who hold positions of authority in this community.

Have compassion on all who suffer from the abuse of power . . . Bring relief to the victims of unjust regimes, and those who are persecuted for their faith or way of life . . . Comfort them in their affliction, and turn the hearts of their oppressors.

Receive in mercy those who have died and no longer exercise or endure worldly government . . . Grant them eternal life in the Kingdom that will not pass away.

We offer our prayers in the name of Christ, King of Kings and Lord of Lords.

Afterword –
On Leading Intercessions

(These notes were appended to the volume Leading Intercessions. *Since some have been kind enough to find them useful they are reprinted here.)*

In most churches today laypeople are invited to lead the intercessions during the Eucharist. It is a responsibility which should be shared as widely as possible. All the Churches have rediscovered the importance of the laity in public worship. They are not simply those who have not been ordained to clerical ministry but the *laos*, the people of God who make up by far the largest order in his Church. A member of the clergy who leads intercessions speaks at that time for the whole Church rather than in the exercise of a special function as at other points in the service.

Here are a few suggestions to aid the intercessor: certainly not ten commandments, but ten points which are worth addressing for this solemn but most joyful ministry.

1 Read the scripture passages for the day. There is sure to be a copy of the lectionary in the church, but it is useful to have a personal copy if you are often called upon for intercessions. Pray for guidance as you prepare for this act of worship.
2 Write down what you want to say, fully or in notes according to your confidence in your own memory. If you use this book it may be best to copy out the words for the day, inserting any special needs in the appropriate places so that everything flows smoothly.
3 Make your intercessions particular by supplementing the suggested forms with specific immediate

matters, local or from the wider world. Consult
with your priest or minister about cases of sickness or other trouble, or recent deaths. Respect
confidentiality: sometimes people do not want
their problems mentioned publicly.

4 Do not make your intercessions too particular.
This is not the time for giving out the weekly
notices, and God does not need all the details. Pray
for 'the next meeting of the Parochial Church
Council' rather than for 'the meeting of the
Parochial Church Council which will be held in
the vestry at 8 on Wednesday evening'; but it
may be good to mention any special matter to be
discussed. Do not try to read out all the names of
members in a group or committee if they are
numerous; apart from being tedious, it is easy to
cause offence by forgetting someone.

5 Avoid voicing personal opinions. By all means
pray for causes or groups which you have at heart,
but do not extol their virtues or the wickedness of
their opponents. We are all sinners and all children
of God who loves us, and the oppressors need our
prayers as much as the oppressed.

6 As well as careful reading of the scripture passages, consider whether there is a particular theme
for the service. The idea of a weekly theme is not
incorporated in the new lectionary, but it is wise to
have a word with the preacher and see if there is
anything that he or she would like picked up in the
intercessions.

7 Do not take too long. Very long intercessions can
lose the devout attention of the congregation and
upset the balance of the service. As a very rough
guide, double the length of the passages offered
in this book should be the maximum. If these
seem sufficient in themselves, with perhaps a few
specific names, there is no need to run on further.

8   Be sure that your speech is clear and audible. Any
    of the clergy, or a trained lay reader, can help here.
    Success comes from clarity and good projection,
    not shouting. Test the acoustics of the church from
    the place where you will be standing: even compe-
    tent and experienced speakers can be caught out
    by a difficult building.

9   Use your natural voice, adapted only as neces-
    sary for being heard by more people. The affected
    'parsonical' voice is, happily, almost extinct and
    needs no lay revival.

10 Despite all these injunctions, accept the duty with
    confidence and joy. Be reverent, but not anxious.
    You are offering prayer to a loving Father, in the
    presence of other Christians. This is, in the most
    wonderful sense, a family occasion.